Drew Provan

Giving Great Presentations

In easy steps is an imprint of In Easy Steps Limited
Southfield Road · Southam
Warwickshire CV47 0FB · United Kingdom
www.ineasysteps.com

Notice of Liability
Every effort has been made to ensure that this book contains accurate
and current information. However, In Easy Steps Limited and the
author shall not be liable for any loss or damage suffered by readers
as a result of any information contained herein.

Trademarks
All trademarks are acknowledged as belonging to their respective
companies.

Printed and bound in the United Kingdom

ISBN-13 978-1-84078-371-1
ISBN-10 1-84078-371-0

Contents

1 Successful Presentation

Presenting information to others is a key skill required in most professions today. Deciding on your message, preparation and practice are the keystones to successful presentation.

The Art of Presentation

"There are two types of speakers: those that are nervous and those that are liars." Mark Twain (1835–1910).

Being invited to give a talk, or present information to colleagues, is both flattering and exhilarating. But the initial euphoria soon wears off and the reality of actually performing fills most people with utter dread. Public speaking is one of the most feared occasions for most people. It would be very unusual to find someone who did not get at least a *little* nervous before standing up in front of an audience. Presenting is very public and all eyes will be on you. This is *your* chance to shine, to show what you know and deliver it well. It can also help determine the outcome of a meeting or negotiation. A great presentation needs to *persuade*. All too often we perform well below our expectations because we are anxious and often badly prepared. Many presenters give little or no thought as to what their slides look like, or how their message will be delivered. Despite the huge sums of money companies spend on advertising and publicity, little is spent on training the workforce to use PowerPoint, or present well. On top of all this, there are the technical aspects which often faze the novice presenter, involving laptops, microphones and lighting.

When we think of presentations, we often imagine erudite professors standing on a stage behind a lectern giving a very formal talk, but we are exposed to slick presentations every day, for example news presenters and chat show hosts on TV. It is a fact of life that in most professions today we are expected to "present", for example:

● Briefing your manager on the progress of a project

● Negotiating your role within a company, possibly seeking a pay rise

● Presenting the latest sales figures or performance targets to your team

- Lecturing on a specialized topic to peers or a lay audience

- Giving research seminars to colleagues

- Invited talks to specialist societies locally, nationally and internationally

- Giving evidence in court

- Giving the best man's speech at a wedding

Secrets of great presentation

We have all listened to speakers who are engaging individuals, who seem totally in control of their audiovisual aids and their mouths! These guys are born presenters, surely? Up to a point this may be true, but most great presenters are at the top of their game because *they work very hard to be there.* They plan meticulously, design their "story" carefully and invest many hours rehearsing so their presentation delivers a clear message. They are also very skillful at constructing slideshows that *complement* their message rather than distract the audience. The bottom line: great presenters inform us but most of all, they *inspire* us!

So, there are no real "secrets" or quick fixes, but rest assured that with practice and planning we can all deliver knockout pitches! But you need to *want* to improve.

But is it art?

Absolutely! This is true showmanship. You could be the most knowledgeable professor who ever lived but if you cannot deliver your message well this is a lost opportunity. Presenting effectively takes much practice. With experience you will improve. Trust me, even if your presentations are clumsy now they will get better. Many of the techniques used by presenters are similar to those by actors in terms of delivery, voice, breathing technique, timing, drama, holding one's frame, all of which give your presentation maximum impact. So this really *is* an art, and one worth working at, since there are few careers that would not benefit from well-honed presentation skills.

We will cover all aspects of presentation technique in the book which, hopefully, will provide guidance which will help shape your talks, aid delivery of your material and boost your confidence.

Hot tip

Delivering a great presentation requires solid planning and extensive rehearsal. Invest time in these areas to ensure your pitch is good.

Keys to Success

Solid preparation is an absolute must. Without this, your presentation will lack clarity and direction, and your message will be lost. Investing substantial amounts of preparation time ahead of your presentation will ensure smooth flow and will also give you the confidence needed which is crucially important if you are to give a persuasive talk.

So what are the components of successful presentation?

Solid preparation
Well ahead of the actual presentation, you need to have a clear idea of what your key messages will comprise. You may be an expert in the field, but it still pays to spend time reviewing what is already known about the topic. Include the latest research findings, especially if this is a fast-moving field. This helps make your talk appear fresh. It also avoids the embarrassment of omitting data that may be known to the audience albeit not known to you!

Connection with the audience
This is a complex area, and includes rapport, empathy and other characteristics. The audience want to like you and for your talk to go well. You need to use eye contact and body language to get your message across and, for some of the information (certainly the key messages), to be learned. If you bore the audience, perhaps through lack of conviction or because you turn your back to them while you read your slides, your message will be lost and the opportunity wasted.

Having a clear message
Are you *absolutely* clear what message you are trying to get across? Is the content fresh? If you are not completely clear then you cannot expect the audience to follow the arguments and come away with some solid key messages. Write down the key points that you want conveyed by your talk, *then* construct your presentation around these. Your presentation needs a story – get this straight and the rest will follow.

Use of appropriate visual aids
Some aids such as computer-generated slides can enhance your presentation, emphasizing key points. Using graphics can convey a great deal of information. However, these aids can become so overbearing that the messages are lost (*this is discussed later in Chapter 6*).

Beware

Make sure you define your key messages before you start to draft your presentation.

Confidence

This is probably your most powerful tool. Mediocre content delivered by a confident presenter may succeed but even the best content delivered by an unconfident presenter will fail.

Conviction

If you have no conviction about the topic or product why should the audience? This characteristic goes hand in hand with confidence. Together they are incredibly powerful, especially when you are aiming to influence the audience's behavior.

Enthusiasm of the speaker

Again, this goes pretty much along with confidence and conviction. Be enthusiastic! It is actually fairly infectious. If you are enthusiastic it will make the audience much more receptive to what you have to say.

Don't forget

Even if your slides are not the best, you can still make a big impression if you deliver with passion.

Ensure your material is relevant to the audience

This goes without saying – or does it? Are you sure the material you are going to present is *actually* what they want to hear?

Planning

Decide on your key messages and plan your presentation around this. Work out, in rough, what material you could use that would help support your key messages. Start early to avoid rushing the process since you risk missing out important material.

Body language

Be assured but not cocky or too smart. The way you stand, move and articulate is picked up by the audience very quickly. Getting this right can make you look very masterful and in control.

Successful question and answer handling

Often a dreaded part of any pitch. You can easily be wrong-footed. This important area is discussed in detail later.

Handouts

People like mementos. Audiences don't mind writing notes but they do not generally possess shorthand skills and they want to listen to you rather than spend their time scribbling notes. Give them good handouts that reinforce your message.

11

Why Have They Asked You?

Unless you have nominated yourself to give this talk (unlikely) then someone has consciously chosen *you* to present. Why might this be?

- You have above-average knowledge of the topic. This is worth remembering when you feel nervous, or that your presentation may not be good enough. It is almost guaranteed that you will know more than the audience about your topic

- You are working in the field and have first-hand experience

- You may be the team leader or a key member of the team with a major role in the project

- People have heard you present before and know you do it well

- Companies often have a "speakers bureau", which is a panel of seasoned key opinion leaders who understand the area well, are respected in their field and are well known to the audience. Speakers like this are often nurtured by companies because they deliver "on-message"

What if you do not feel qualified?

If you honestly feel you cannot present on the chosen topic you must say so. Although you may feel flattered to be asked, you do not want to stand up in front of an audience and talk about subjects that are foreign or unfamiliar. You will give the game away when it comes to Questions and Answers, and you will lose credibility. In these situations it is better to decline politely and offer one or two names of experienced speakers if you have colleagues who would be better placed than you to deliver the presentation, or suggest a topic you *can* talk about confidently.

What is Expected From You?

This is the most fundamental question to ask yourself when invited to give a presentation: *"What do they want to know?"*

What is the title of your presentation?

Do you understand it? Sometimes titles can be cryptic so if you are not sure what the title means – ask!

The agenda

There is an agenda to every meeting, conference or telephone conference. Are you clear you know what this is?

If you are presenting sales figures to your local team at work, for example, then the remit of your talk will be very obvious.

Is this part of a conference program?

If you are presenting in a session with other speakers are you clear about what they will be talking about? This helps avoid the embarrassment of having slides similar to your co-presenters. It makes you look sloppy and the audience will construe this as a speaker who has not bothered to find out what he or she is meant to be doing and making sure it fits in with his or her co-presenters' material. Confer with your co-presenters early on. Arrange a telephone conference to discuss the areas you each wish to cover.

Delivery

Delivery of material to colleagues round a table is very different to speaking to several hundred delegates at a conference. How will you deliver your presentation?

Are they expecting interaction?

This works with small groups, possibly up to 50 people, but once the audience rises to 60 and beyond this becomes very difficult. I have seen speakers try to take questions during their speech only to find they cannot hear the question properly and the whole experience becomes quite embarrassing.

Length of presentation

How many minutes is your talking time and how long do you have for questions? You must bear this in mind when you plan your presentation. Audiences are very unforgiving when it comes to speakers that overrun their time slot, especially if it leaves little time for questions. It is far better to finish early – audiences never seem to complain about this!

Hot tip

Talk to the organizers and clarify the objectives of your presentation.

Don't forget

Find out how long you are speaking for and how many minutes you have for Q & A.

Formal Presentations

Formal presentations are often major events or conferences. They allow people to showcase their expertise and it is an exciting opportunity. But people are often scared of formal talks, largely because the timings are strict, the audience is an unknown commodity, and the fear of failure or something going wrong gets the adrenalin flowing! Invitations are generally sent out many months ahead with *potentially* lots of preparation time. However, human nature being what it is, we often leave the writing of our talks until fairly close to the date of the event! This leads to panic, poor slide design, and an overall state of anxiety.

The net effect of all this leads to a suboptimal performance which makes us very wary of accepting an invitation next time. This vicious cycle can be broken by learning to present well – this will boost your confidence and make you more likely to present again and become even better!

However, it need not be like this. As with all presentations, large and small, get the following straight:

- What is the structure of the session?

- Who are the speakers?

- What are they covering in their talks?

- What is the title of your slot and exactly what do they want from your presentation?

- Research the audience, their experience and their expectations

- How long is your presentation and how many minutes have they allowed for questions?

- Do they want your slides in advance of the meeting? Quite often they will ask for finished slides two or more weeks ahead of the conference in order to allow time for printing

- Do you need to bring your presentation on CD ROM, flash disk or on another format?

- Are they providing all the audiovisual support? Some speakers like to use their own laptops for presenting but this can cause further unforeseen problems

- Are they printing handouts or must you supply these?

Informal Presentations

People are less anxious when asked to give informal presentations. However, you should take the same care as you would for a formal presentation. In fact, the informal events may be *more* error-prone than formal presentations because:

- You are more relaxed when you plan

- You are also more relaxed when you present

- You may leave the writing and slide design until close to the event and end up rushing the process

- Slides and other audiovisual aids may be imperfect but you feel you can muddle through

- Your audience is much more likely to challenge statements (and heckle!) than in the formal setting when they might be more inhibited

- You can see the audience up close and this is often more stress-inducing than addressing a faceless mass of people

Beware

Avoid being too relaxed or you may be caught unawares. Informal presentations require planning, too.

As with the formal event, make sure you are absolutely clear what they want you to cover, for how long, whether it can be interactive, should you bring handouts or will the organizers print these for you, do they need your slides in advance or are they expecting you to use a white board or flip chart?

Usually you do not have to send your slides in advance and can take them to the meeting on a USB flash disk. You can also probably use your own laptop for the presentation.

Dress code
What do you wear if your audience is going to be dressed in T-shirts and jeans? Should you wear the same? For these events smart-casual may be reasonable, or even smarter – wear your normal business clothes. This will give you more confidence and style and will separate you from the audience (unless you are an audience member who is taking part in a session where several audience members are expected to present, in which case it would be better to conform to their dress code).

By dressing smartly the audience is more likely to take you and your messages seriously. You will have more gravitas if you appear smartly dressed and in control.

The Audience

The audience is key. The event is *about* them and *for* them. Your presentation must be designed with the audience in mind.

This is what can make or break your confidence, in many ways. Get it right and the whole event will be rewarding and you will be keen to do it again, but if the audience is lukewarm or even worse, hostile, it can put you off ever getting up on stage again!

Do some research on the audience – find out as much as you can about them. This will ensure you tailor your presentation better.

Consider:

- Who are you addressing?

- What is their level of knowledge?

- What do they know about the subject you are talking about?

- How many of them are there?

- If you are presenting technical or other specialized information to a lay (non-specialized) audience try to avoid over-use of jargon otherwise you will lose them

- If you are presenting to peers then the use of jargon is expected, and you should not "dumb down" your talk

- What is their native language? If it is not English you will need to simplify your slides and your speech. You will also need to use less slides because each one will take longer to present

- What do the audience expect to gain from your presentation? Are they expecting to hear the latest advances in the field? Are they looking to you to provide direction to help them carry out their job? Do they expect you to provide your opinions or to be non-judgmental?

- Does this audience have strong views one way or the other? This is useful to know in advance since it helps you develop your pitch

- Could there be resistance from the audience? They might not want to follow your key messages

- What style of presentation would suit this audience? You want to be able to reach the audience but the format of the presentation might prevent this. Would a relaxed interactive talk be preferable to one where you stand behind a lectern for one hour giving a didactic lecture?

- If you have co-presenters make sure you know what they will be covering otherwise you may end up duplicating information and the audience will be disappointed

Beware

If you are one of a group of presenters, coordinate with your co-presenters to ensure your talk does not overlap with theirs.

17

Key Messages

These define your presentation. If there is no key message then it is hardly worth the effort of getting up to speak. But I would hope you do have key messages and the aim should be to make these as obvious and unambiguous as possible.

The key messages should provide focus to your presentation.

Decide on your ending before you start writing
This is the punchline. Once you have decided what this is, you can create your presentation since you know where you want to get to by the end of the presentation.

Tell them what the key points are right upfront
That will help them focus on what you say later, and helps them understand why you are showing them particular graphs, charts or other information.

Repeat the key points again at the end
This helps reinforce the message and with any luck these will be the points they will remember long after the event is over.

Hot tip

Write the conclusions before you draft the rest of the speech. The content should match the conclusions.

You are aiming to influence behavior or opinion
If the presentation is scientific the key messages are generally related to how something works or happens, and the evidence backing up your statement will make up much of the talk.

If your presentation relates to company or team performance then your key messages will relate to specific robust data to back up your statements.

Keep the messages simple but not simplistic
Elaborate words and fancy graphics will fail if your message is not clear.

You don't need many key messages
It is probably best to have 3 or 4 key points that you want the audience to retain after the presentation has ended. Skillful engineering of your speech and slides will help this happen.

Keep it relevant
Let them know who the key message is for (them), what they will do as a result of hearing the key messages (work better, harder, be more engaged with the company), and why the message will alter behavior.

Don't overdo the graphics
They may look great on your PC but when shown to an audience they may look conceited and simply there for effect (style over substance). They also make it harder for the audience to grasp the key concepts of your speech.

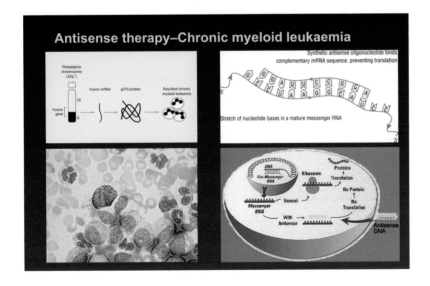

Beware

Too many graphics or highly complex graphics may spoil a good presentation.

Gauging Your Performance

How can you tell if your presentation has been well-received? Sure, they will applaud at the end, but what other clues are there? Maybe you could count the number of people on the front row  who fall asleep or yawn during your talk (this does happen, and it can be quite disconcerting but don't take it too personally).

Conferences and other staged events often use feedback forms where the audience can rate each speaker, their presentation content, delivery and other factors. These can be useful, particularly to the organizers, since they will not be likely to invite a bad speaker back again. So if you receive a regular stream of invites to speak then take this as a measure of your stage appeal.

A better method of determining whether you have had any impact might be whether people can recall your key messages, and whether what you have said has any influence on their behavior.

If you have presented information to your team it will be fairly obvious whether your presentation has had any bearing on the way they work, or on the way they think about specific areas of their work.

For large meetings, it may be more difficult to tell whether your message has sunk in, but there may be ways in which to tell. You may feel a specific practice is outdated and should be changed. You will have shown them why you think this, and you will have provided a key message about how you think it would be done better. From publications and talking to people you may notice that practice has indeed changed, moving towards your view.

If your talk has been motivational does your team now appear to be better motivated? Do they work better, or complain less?

If your talk was intended to bring all team members up to the same level so they work better together, does this appear to be the case?

Presentation Pitfalls

Like me, you must have sat through some pretty tedious presentations, with the speaker droning on whilst you either fall asleep, or start sending text messages on your cell phone. A bad speaker can make time appear to stand still!

Audiences tend to judge the speaker within the first few minutes of the start of a presentation, and if they judge you badly initially, it is very difficult to recover.

So what do audiences dislike?

- Fumbling awkward starts

- Apologetic speakers who make excuses about not having enough time to cover the subject properly

- Speakers who do not start on time or who finish late

- Presentations with no clear purpose and which fail to communicate well

- Speakers who read their slides to the audience

- Speakers who use too many slides

- Presenters who talk very quickly

- Slides with too much information or text that is difficult to read

- Poor quality graphics

- Cheesy animations, backgrounds or other gratuitous effects

- Speakers who turn their back on the audience or who do not engage with their audience

- Speakers who cannot control their AV equipment, pressing the back key instead of advance on the slides

- Bad, racist or sexist jokes

- Poor laser pointer control

- Skipping over "superfluous" slides (why are those slides in there at all?)

- Cartoons or graphics with no relevance to text on the slide

Beware

There are many clearly defined pitfalls when presenting. Be aware of these and avoid making them.

Summary

- In most professions you will be called on to give presentations from time to time

- At other times, such as weddings, leaving parties and other events, you may be asked to give a speech

- Learning good presentation technique is therefore useful in your personal as well as professional life

- Presenting well is not innate but takes skill, practice and determination

- Nervousness and anxiety are common and to be expected. The more presentations you give, the better you get and this will help to build your confidence

- Investing time in researching your topic is essential

- Decide on your key messages early on and construct your presentation around these

- What you say must be relevant to the audience. Resist the temptation to reuse slide decks or previous speeches. "One size fits all" does not work

- Rehearse your presentation several times before the big day and remove any unnecessary information from your slides. Simplicity is preferable to highly complex visuals

- Seek feedback on your performance and learn from any mistakes you make

- With practice you will fear presentations less, start to channel your nervousness, and begin to enjoy the challenge

- Learning to present well can only enhance your career, and bad presentations can lose you a sale and hinder your career progress!

2 Solid Foundations

Successful presentations require good content, which must be researched, planned and delivered in a logical order. Presentations should be tailor-made for each audience and must deliver the anticipated content.

What Makes a Great Presenter?

We have all sat through hundreds of presentations but we probably cannot recall very many of them. But we can remember the really good ones – why? What was it about those presentations that make them stick in our minds? The topic? Probably partially, but usually it is the *presenter*. There are many tools a good presenter uses that make his or her speech truly memorable. Often the techniques used are quite subtle but are highly effective nonetheless.

Enthusiasm

This goes hand in hand with passion. If the presenter has no real enthusiasm for the subject then why should the audience? Great presenters are generally very fired up and transmit this passion to the audience. It's infectious! We are far more likely to remain attentive when listening to someone who actually cares deeply about the business, product, software or treatment they are presenting than someone who is simply going through the motions.

Enjoys presenting to an audience

"Enjoys" may seem an odd word for something you might view as scary! Presenters who have been performing in front of audiences have the ability to make it look as though they are enjoying the occasion even when they are not. It is easy to forget that we all get nervous, even experienced TV presenters or actors. But once the show starts the nerves tend to abate quickly and you can really enjoy talking to your audience, particularly if you get off to a strong start.

Entertains

We all love to be entertained. It makes the presentation come to life and generally helps reinforce the speaker's key messages. By entertaining the audience you help them remember *you,* as well as your story and its messages.

Story

This is closely linked with entertainment. A good talk should have a beginning, a middle and an end, just like any good story. When these sections of the presentation are clear it makes the story line easy to follow. The beginning and the end are where the key messages are conveyed and reinforced. Give them anecdotes, examples from your own business to bring the presentation to life. This turns an abstract presentation into something living and real.

Voice factor

Your voice should be audible to all members of the audience, and speech should be clear but delivered more slowly than normal conversational speech. This makes sure people can follow what you say, and also avoids you rushing through complex data. A good speaker will avoid talking in a monotone, and will vary the pitch throughout the talk to keep it sounding interesting.

Body language and positioning

Great presenters are comfortable walking around the stage, sometimes standing behind the lectern. This gives them a relaxed look which relaxes the audience. You would never see a good speaker gripping the lectern with both hands throughout their talk. This would convey major anxiety! We will cover aspects of body language later.

Timing

Even if there is a lot of information to convey, a good speaker will pace the talk correctly, with pauses between sections. The experienced speaker will vary the pace in order to add to the interest and entertainment of the presentation.

Inclusivity

It's not about "us and them" – the good speaker will want to make the audience feel *involved*.

Humility

Even if the speaker is very senior or rated top of his or her profession they will often be self-effacing, even humble. This endears them to the audience and makes them more receptive.

Props

A savvy speaker will make judicious use of PowerPoint or other aids to convey the message. They will not overdo their use since less is definitely more.

Finale

A great presenter has the skill to tie all the threads of the story together in a conclusion that will be memorable long after the show is over. This is the part you really want them to remember, even if they cannot recall the rest of the pitch.

Beware

Monotonous tones will make even the most interesting subject appear dull. Learn how to use your voice.

Things to Avoid

Some presentations are just plain irritating and often you wish you were somewhere else doing something useful rather than listening to a bad presenter. Although the audience will want you to succeed, they will decide within the first 30 seconds whether it is worth listening to you or tuning out!

Avoid:

- Starting or ending late. This shows a lack of respect for the audience

- Failing to be introduced or to provide your own introduction. Make sure the audience know who you are and who or what you represent

- Presentations with no obvious focus

- Appearing bored. Why should they pay attention to you if you appear to be lacking passion and enthusiasm?

- Speaking softly or not standing close enough to the microphone

- Ad libbing too much (some improvisation is essential but try not to construct your talk in front of a live audience)

- Standing totally still – it is essential to move around a little

- Not making eye contact with the audience

- Self-criticism or apologies

- Don't criticize others either! It will reflect badly on *you*, not them

- Holding laser pointer at screen too long; any nervous tremor will be very obvious

- Heavy use of unfamiliar jargon or abbreviations – one sure fire way of losing the audience!

- Overloading your audience with information – it is always tempting to include as much information as possible in a presentation but it is far better to stay focused (less is more)

- Text-heavy slides – the audience will attempt to read these and will not be listening to what you have to say

- Too many slides – this is seen more often with inexperienced or unconfident speakers who want *all* their information to be available and shown

- Small fonts – the text cannot be read and the audience will be very irritated

- Too many colors make the slides look garish and difficult to read

- Animation effects. These were fashionable a few years back with animations in the templates which moved each time a new slide was shown. Some people even use animated graphics on the slides but unless these are crucial to the content (such as looking at a video of cells dividing or a piece of machinery in action) avoid them

- Irrelevant information, stories or jokes

- Reading from notes or (far worse) a script. Reading verbatim is totally discouraged. It's a bit like being read a bedtime story!

- Talking in a monotone

- Keeping your hands in your pockets or playing with your hair

Beware

Don't use too much jargon and avoid text-heavy visuals.

Answer The Question!

Some people fail exams because they don't know their stuff. Others fail, *not* because they are not bright, but because they fail to answer the examiner's question. They sometimes do this because they feel unconfident, and rather than expose this, they include everything they know about a subject even if it's not totally relevant to the question being asked. This will annoy the examiner who will award a lower mark than if the candidate had stuck to the question that was asked.

The same is true of presentations. I attended one recently where a senior colleague was addressing a large audience on a very specific topic. Although it was a subject area in which he is well known, he is actually more interested in a different research area so he devoted most of his time to that instead. The audience was angry since many had come specifically to hear the presentation as billed on the program. Because he failed to speak on the scheduled subject, about half of the audience walked out. His back was to the audience the whole time (very poor technique) so he failed to notice, sadly.

Long before you give your talk, make sure you have clarified the expectations with the organizers. Do not leave this till the day before.

What is the title of your talk?

Do you understand it? Is it something you can speak about? If not, decline or suggest an alternative topic. Some titles can be ambiguous – rephrase it if necessary.

Who decides the title?

Is this something an organizer has provided for you, which cannot be changed, or can you make up your own title? If so, make it as broad but interesting as you can. Make sure it encompasses the subject area you want to talk about.

The hidden agenda

If you are giving an internal presentation to colleagues then there should be no hidden agenda behind your talk. Sometimes when consultants or external advisors are asked to give talks by companies there may be specific points they want you to cover. For example, they may want you to highlight failings of rival companies whilst emphasizing the positives about the company you represent. There may be information they do *not* want you

Beware

Failure to deliver the expected content in a speech will leave the audience disappointed.

to disclose. Check with the organizers whether you are free to include any information you wish or whether your presentation has to be reviewed by the company in question (this is fairly common practice).

How to get it right

- What is the title of your presentation? Are you happy with that? If not, discuss with the person who invited you and change it!

- Are you clear about what they want you to cover? If not, ask now, before you put pen to paper. Of course, make sure you do not include any material that your co-presenters will be covering. If you are not sure what their presentation is about – ask them

- Are your key messages assembled? Decide on these upfront. Do this early

- Draft your presentation based on the key messages

- Incorporate relevant facts, statistics, and graphs

- Keep it as simple as you can. It may be tempting to try to blow the audience away with fancy graphics and lots of data and text, but your message will be lost. The best talks have very simple graphics and little text. It should be your spoken message that captivates them and makes the key messages clear

- Do the key messages fit with the title? Will this fit with the audience's expectation from your talk? If in doubt, redesign your key messages

- Have you got the information needed to provide the story which will lead to your conclusions and finale? If not, try to find this by talking to colleagues

- Search the Internet for related material to see if anything in your presentation is contradictory or wrong

- Later, stand back and think: *given the title of this presentation am I completely sure I am answering the question, and is this what my audience expects to hear?* If it is not, rework the speech, or slides, until anything irrelevant has been removed

Hot tip

Search the Internet for material relevant to your talk.

Know Your Material

Once you have decided on your presentation title and you have assembled the key messages which you want the audience to retain, you will need to start gathering information.

You may be an expert in the subject area, or it may be something you know little about. Either way, you need to pull together information from a number of sources and construct a presentation that will be interesting, informative and hopefully inspirational! One would imagine that being a real expert must be a major advantage when it comes to presenting, but sometimes it can work against you. Experts can sometimes gloss over topics that are not well known to the audience assuming that they will follow all the arguments. Preparing a presentation on something you know little about forces you to research the field more thoroughly since most of it is unknown to you.

How much information do you need?
Generally you should gather more information than you need or will present. You can discard the irrelevant or redundant information later.

When to start the preparation
As soon as you accept the invitation it is a good idea to peruse journals and books for material which you may include in your presentation. It is much better to plan ahead and have everything ready well ahead of the presentation date, especially since conference organizers may ask for your slides two weeks before the meeting. Human nature being what it is, and because we are busy, people often leave things till the last minute and reuse old slide decks or borrow other people's.

Recycling your previous presentations
This could be a real timesaver but the risks are:

- The material will not be fresh

- Some material may obviously be obsolete

- The audience demographics on this occasion may differ from that previously

- The presentation may not have worked well last time

- You may not have corrected errors from last time

Beware

Reusing old presentations saves time but is not advised. The end result is generally poor.

30

Locating information for the presentation

For internal meetings, project team meetings, sales updates and similar, you probably have most of the information you need or can ask a colleague for data and charts for your presentation.

For conferences or external meetings you can get information from textbooks (although these are out of date as soon as they get into print), journals, or books of notable quotations.

Locating presentations on the Internet

Although I would not suggest you use someone else's presentation, you can learn from these so I would suggest that if you are completely stuck for ideas do a Google search and include ":ppt" in the search string. For example, to find PowerPoint files relating to "energy saving" type "energy saving:ppt" into the Google search box.

Hot tip

The Internet is a great place to find images for presentations. Learn how to refine your searches to minimize the amount of junk you obtain.

Plan Your Story

Good presentations must have a story. Get this right and you're more than half way there. Without a story your presentation will be aimless and weak, and will fail to make an impact.

Like all stories there should be a:

1 Beginning

2 Middle

3 End

Beginning

This is your *Introduction* which aims to get their attention early. If the beginning is strong you will keep their attention (the reverse is also true, and weak fumbling starts tend to lose the audience). You can be dramatic here, for example by providing a powerful statistic:

"Did you know that over 50% of small businesses fail in the first year and 95% fail within the first five years?"

Alternatively you can recite an anecdote or possibly, if you are very confident, tell a joke (although joke are probably best avoided).

In this section you are telling them what you are going to tell them. You should whet their appetite – you want to make sure they listen to the entire presentation.

Middle

The main body of the talk is the largest section. Here you will deliver the main story which will provide the facts and figures required to reach your conclusion. Since this is the largest section it will need to be subdivided into smaller chunks. This will make the whole story much easier to follow. The subsections should flow in a logical order.

You need to work on your arguments, making sure these are consistent and support your claims or conclusions. Use data tables, charts, or other graphics to complement what you say. If anything appears redundant, remove it.

Try to use real case examples since this helps put what you are saying into real world context and people will be able to grasp the concept more quickly.

Try to keep your talk as fresh as possible by using as much up-to-date information as you can find.

End

Finally you will reach the *Conclusion* which draws together all the threads you have developed through the main body of the talk. If you are giving a PowerPoint presentation keep your conclusions to one slide, and keep it as punchy (brief) as possible. Seeing "*Conclusion 1, Conclusion 2*, etc." is off-putting and suggests you cannot focus your ideas succinctly enough.

Advantages of structuring your presentation

Having the three main sections is useful because it:

- Adds interest

- Helps maintain the audience's attention

- Assists understanding

- Makes your messages much more memorable

Don't forget

A great Conclusion slide will emphasize your key messages and tie everything together.

33

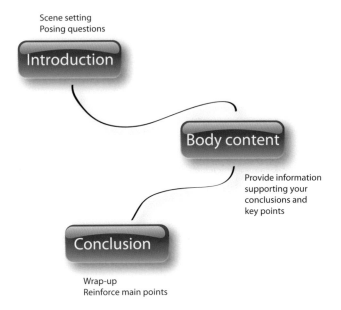

Scene setting
Posing questions

Introduction

Body content

Provide information supporting your conclusions and key points

Conclusion

Wrap-up
Reinforce main points

Grab Their Attention Early!

The first few minutes of any presentation are critical to the success of the whole show. They set the stage and tone for your presentation. If what you say in the first few minutes does not excite them, then they will probably pay less attention to what you say later.

The whole process begins after the introducer says *"And now I would like to welcome John Doe to talk to us about his latest study of whatever"*.

At this point you are probably sitting in the front row wishing you were somewhere else, anywhere else but here! You need to appear relaxed and confident, walking onto the stage or towards the lectern briskly. Try to scan some of the faces in the audience and smile. This helps build your confidence and also helps develop anticipation within the audience. Here is someone who looks comfortable in this setting and is going to deliver a good presentation.

How to start?

Avoid long preambles, but do thank the organizers or whoever invited you to talk. Let them know you are delighted to be given this opportunity to share your thoughts on whatever your subject will be, present your latest research data, and so on.

This should take no more than a minute or two and should lead into the main introduction. This is the part of your presentation where you set out your stall and let them know exactly what they should expect to hear when you give the main part of the talk. It lets the audience know that this information is for *them*, designed with this audience in mind. You will also tell them about the key messages you wish to share with them. Use phrases like *"I will share with you some of our latest research findings, after which you will be able to see why a change in approach is necessary for..."*, *"I will show you how we changed our sales strategy six months ago, and how this is now paying dividends with sales up by forty percent"*, or something similar.

If you want to tell them about your strategy for reducing hospital-acquired infection you could say something like *"My main research focus is hospital-acquired infection, and in this thirty minute presentation I will share our latest research findings and suggest ways in which we can reduce such infections by ninety percent."*

"I am one of the VPs of Company X. We have a long and successful track record in the manufacturing of widgets. Today I will share with you our R & D strategy which includes some very innovative new technologies."

Dramatic openers
You may prefer to go for a more dramatic opening statement or questions

"Did you know that...?"

"Until recently we believed that ... In this short presentation I will show you why these assumptions are incorrect and ..."

"Have you ever wondered why/if...?"

"Generally X disease is regarded as a benign disorder. Let me tell you about Mary, a 24-year-old secretary, who suffered near-fatal consequences of this disease. I will show you why in certain individuals X disease is not benign."

Hopefully once you have got through the first couple of minutes and grabbed their attention, the rest of the talk will flow smoothly.

Hot tip

Make your presentation personal. Use stories and dramatic openers.

35

Engage The Audience

There is no doubt that presenting in public is both intimidating and stressful. You might feel like the audience is the "enemy" but really they are on your side. They have given up their time and are prepared to sit through your presentation hoping to learn from it. The audience will regard you as an expert in the subject of your presentation, and they will look up to you as someone who has the answers. In effect, they have a major vested interest in your success – they do *not* want you to fail.

But it must be remembered that this is about them (the audience) and not you, irrespective of how you feel inside. You have done your homework, researched the topic, constructed the slides, all for them. You must focus on their needs and make them feel valued.

Customize
You may have recycled a previous talk or written this one from scratch, but you must avoid making it totally generic. Bring in examples from their business, town, city or product where possible. This helps the audience see how your words relate to them.

Attention!
Two areas are worth noting here:

1. You *must* give 100% to the audience. Irrespective of how many calls you have to make, or other problems you may have, these must be put to one side while you are presenting. If you appear distracted or not fully engaged the audience will pick this up quickly and lose interest

2. The attention span of the audience is not infinite. Adults can remain attentive for 15 to 20 minutes, after which they start to lose this. For some people it may be even shorter

Keep it short
Most people when presenting will use their whole allotted time and many will even run over. This is a sign of a presenter who has paid little attention to the task, time allowed and the audience. It is very disrespectful to your colleague presenters and to the audience, to overrun your time slot. It means the question time is reduced and the next speaker, if there is one, will have to start his or her talk late. So don't overrun!

Beware

Try to engage the audience – grab their attention so they listen to the whole story.

Use less time than you have been allotted

Rather than use your whole time allocation, keep your talk simple and short. If you have been given 30 minutes, use 20 or maybe 25 then stop. The audience will *never* complain about a shorter presentation!

The lectern is not a life raft

Talks are often given using a lectern, a stand on the stage with a light, microphone and laptop or keyboard for advancing your slides. Most formal occasions such as conferences, use these. They are useful as an anchor and place of safety for you. The lectern provides a useful defence for you but at the same time it becomes a *barrier* between you and the audience. To make matters worse, these are often placed to the right or left of the stage. When the lights go down all that the audience can see is your slides, and your voice becomes a voice-over. You might as well be in another city giving the talk! You need to get involved and move around the stage.

Beware

Don't cling to the lectern or podium – it is a barrier between you and the audience.

The most successful presenters who give awe-inspiring talks never stand behind the lectern. Instead they move around all over the stage, engaging the audience, almost having a conversation with them rather than talking *at* them from behind a wall.

You may not feel comfortable or confident doing this but try to move away from the lectern a little each time you talk. See if you can move towards the centre of the stage for a while then go back to the lectern. Eventually you will be able to give your entire talk without having to hide behind the barrier.

Seek Opportunities to Present

Hot tip

Practice as often as you can. Use different locations – the car, the bath tub, shower, elevator. Practice out loud.

Great presenting technique is not innate. It is a skill that comes slightly easier to some people than to others, but even the smoothest and most inspiring presenters have worked very hard to attain their high levels of showmanship. It may seem daunting initially, especially if faced with a large audience, but there are many ways in which you can take your expertise to a new level.

Like playing piano, violin or any other performing art, we improve the more we play. Presenting is very much an art and it, too, relies on practice.

Practice alone

You will write your presentation alone (usually) and will be going through the text in your head but you need to speak *aloud* and to other people in order to see if what you plan to say actually makes sense. Often, text on a slide appears to make sense but when spoken during a presentation you cannot recall what it means, or maybe it contradicts something on an earlier slide. Practice and rehearsal are very much part of the whole process and without these, your timing will likely fail, and your message may be lost.

Practice in small groups

Presenting data at work is a great opportunity to put yourself in the hot seat. Many professions have regular meetings with updates on project workflow, deliverables, sales, research projects and other subjects. Volunteer to present the latest data or update to your team. This requires you to plan and write your presentation and, very often, put together some sort of visual, such as PowerPoint or Keynote slides.

Larger groups

Now we are getting to audiences of 50 or more. This might be a national meeting, perhaps a specialist society or group meeting for all people within a certain industry from all over the country or world. These meetings are usually designed to get people together, to update them on global operations and forecasts. Speaking at these meetings is a golden opportunity to get your ideas across to a large group. This can be quite daunting if you have never done it, but you will get a real buzz when it goes well.

Very large groups

Audiences of 1,000 or more are not uncommon at large international conferences. These presentations are best made by people with experience since the scale of the event can lead to major anxiety! Often the timetable is tight with strict timing, for example 15 minutes for the presentation with 5 minutes for a Question and Answer session. The ability to project yourself and get your ideas across to a large audience is something we all aspire to. Careful preparation and meticulous attention to timing are required. If you can manage this you can manage anything! If you regularly present to smaller audiences and gain in confidence, you will eventually manage to handle larger audiences. Talking to large audiences will be covered later in the book.

 Beware

Presenting to very large groups takes practice and experience. Start with smaller groups and build your confidence.

Summary

- Great presenters are great because they have invested time and energy into their presentations, making sure the content is accurate, easily understood, and appropriate for the audience. They engage their audiences in a conversational journey leading to a high-impact finale. Their presentations are memorable and inspiring

- Good presentations require enthusiasm and passion. If you are not enthusiastic about your topic why should the audience be?

- Early engagement with the audience is essential, you need to make them feel included. Talk *to* them and not *at* them

- The audience will judge you within the first one or two minutes of your presentation so make the *Introduction* strong

- Grab their attention early by making a bold statement or asking a question. Be as dramatic as you feel able. Some people are natural exhibitionists whilst others are fairly quiet. Do what feels natural to you

- Keep your message short and to the point

- Your presentation should have a beginning, middle and end

- Decide on the ending (which will contain your key messages) and write the story around this

- Keep your content fresh and uncluttered

- Keep the number of fonts and colors to a minimum and use clear graphics in place of text where possible

- Learn to entertain and avoid monotones

- Stay on topic or the audience will be disappointed

- Adequate research and planning are critical

- Make sure you start on time and finish on time. It may be an advantage to use only 80–90% of your allotted time

- Practice presenting as much as possible to peers and colleagues. Then move on to larger audiences and eventually you will be able to perform in front of thousands

3 Preparation is Key

Preparation is crucial if you want to make an impression. Software tools such as outliners or mind mapping programs can help you organize your thoughts.

Prepare Yourself

Preparation for a presentation is probably the most important part of the process. Fail to get this right and the presentation may suffer. Preparation includes the mental aspects as well as the organizational.

Mental checklist

- Why you? Are you equipped to do this presentation? Is it a subject area you know well?

- Have you got the time required for this, not just on the day but in terms of research, planning – or are you overcommitted? Many hours of work are required for even a short presentation

- Title and subject to present

- Time allotted

- Audience, and their knowledge background

- Expectations of you

- Your key messages

- How best to tell the story

Organize your thoughts: focus

Many people, when preparing a presentation, rush straight to the PC and trawl through websites looking for information related to their forthcoming presentation. While this is not a *bad* idea, it does not help early on. The downside of computer searches is that the information is too diffuse, and if you want to get your key messages across you must focus.

Switch your computer off or find a quiet space with as few distractions as possible. Grab a notepad and pen and write down your ideas for the talk. Jot down anything that comes into your mind. You can discard most of these, but it helps get the thought processes going!

Ask yourself

- In a nutshell, what exactly am I covering in this presentation? What two or three messages do I want the audience to remember?

- Write down the key messages on a sheet of paper and keep these near you

- Then start jotting down ideas related to the key messages and interlink these, building your story along the way

- You can do a storyboard or use index cards to put a couple of words relating to what you will cover in each slide, if you are giving a PowerPoint presentation

Hot tip

Jot down thoughts in a notebook or on index cards. Use these later to write your talk.

- If your presentation is for 30 minutes, the general rule often cited is 1 slide per minute but you may want to use fewer or more depending on what is on the slides and how long you will be showing each slide as you give your presentation. Rules are meant to be broken so you may only want to use ten slides or maybe many more

Introduction
Who I am
What I do
What I want to share with you

Main body of presentation
Key facts
Data supporting
Ideas
Plans etc.

Conclusions
Key point 1
Key point 2
Key point 3

Place the cards in order

After you have written the skeleton outline of your presentation, making sure you have drafted a strong story with the key messages made clear, then you can get online and start looking for facts, figures and graphics that support your slides.

You may have some old slide decks from which you can copy diagrams, charts and other visuals rather than look for fresh ones. It is best not to simply modify an old set of slides since the story you told last time is going to force you down that same road again, even if subconsciously.

Get Organized

Getting your thoughts organized is mission critical for a solid presentation. By now you will have tons of hand-written notes, web clippings, photos or other artwork. Most of this will be discarded, otherwise you risk overloading your presentation.

Keep bearing in mind:

- The attention span of the audience (short, maybe 15 minutes)

- Control of information overload

- Less is definitely more

Where to start?

You need a plan for your presentation. It should have the 3 components discussed earlier:

- *The beginning* (which will introduce the topic and let the audience know what you will be discussing)

- *The middle* (which is the main body of the presentation). Here you will be able to provide the information the audience needs to understand your key messages

- *The end.* This is a very short section which drives home the key essential elements you want the audience to remember and act on

Tools available

There are many ways to organize your thoughts and your presentation. Those used most commonly are:

1. Paper-based systems, such as sheets of paper, index cards or Post-it notes. This is an analog system but one which has been used for many years. It requires no power or high tech equipment. To use this method it is best to write the beginning and end of the presentation on separate pieces of paper then place these either side of you. For a 30 minute presentation you need about 20 blank pieces of paper, or index cards. Each of these will represent a PowerPoint slide. You then need to break the middle section down into around 3 subsections, which would be around 8 or 9 slides. You cannot assume the audience knows as much as you, so you would provide some background information for them. This would be

the first subsection. The next part of the middle section is where you show them facts and figures and finally, the last part of the body of the talk would be devoted to pulling this together into some kind of analysis. Ultimately you lead them through the conclusions which will hammer home the key points

2 Software solutions. Maybe you are more comfortable working on the computer. You could use a word processing package such as Microsoft Word or something similar. Alternatively there are simple text editors that will do the job just as well. Start by creating 20 or 30 fresh pages (introduce 30 page breaks). Work in print preview mode and use each new page as one slide in your presentation. Start adding the headings of your slides to the pages in the word processor then build the rest of the slide up around this. Copy and paste the "slides" around until you are happy with the order. The downside of this approach is that it often creates sloppy slides and probably does not save you much time. Computers are not particularly helpful when you are trying to be creative, although many people do type their novels, presentations, memoirs or blogs straight into a computer program. So if this works for you – fine, do it that way

3 Start keeping a wallet folder with documents, clippings, reprints and other bits of information that might be useful for your talk. Much of it might be junk but you can discard that later. It is better to have excess material than insufficient

4 Start collecting graphs, photographs, line art and other possible images to add to your slides. Keep these in a folder marked with the name of your presentation. Alternatively, there are software programs that let you collect material for use later. Examples include Extensis Portfolio, Microsoft Expression Media or the free online resource Evernote. Again, it is better to have a large catalog of images from which you can choose the most suitable and highest quality for your presentation

Hot tip

Keep a wallet file (or computer folder) for text, image and web clippings.

Mind Mapping

Sometimes it is difficult to know what information you should include in a presentation. You may have lots of ideas in your head but cannot organize these. Mind mapping is a technique which helps develop ideas, including presentations. Mind mapping can be carried out on paper but there are several programs available that help you map things out. The danger of using this type of software is that you get so immersed in the details that you may find it difficult to draw out the threads of your story.

Mind mapping works by creating a central point which would be "Presentation" and branches are drawn out to represent various levels of the presentation. You might draw a branch for "Introduction", another for "Main Body of Presentation" and a third for the "Conclusions". The software works in a similar way to scribbling down notes on a sheet of paper. The advantages are that items can be moved around from section to section. In this way, all your information ends up where it should be and you can get a good overview of what material you need for your presentation. When it comes time to draft the presentation you can also use the mind maps to help you structure your talks.

When you are mind mapping, moving items around helps build relationships between sections of your presentation. This will help you see relevant and irrelevant pieces of your argument. The process may also suggest new ideas to bring in to help your story and its flow. But beware you are not dazzled by the software and get bogged down.

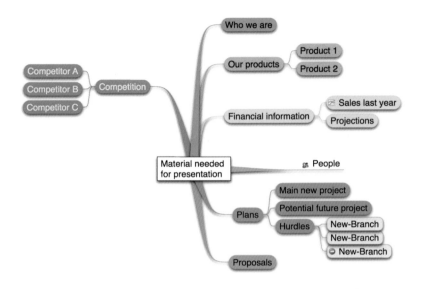

This example shows a simplified plan of a presentation. Different parts are given separate colors to make them more obvious.

The example below shows a simplified version of a presentation showing its main parts (*Introduction*, *Main Body* and *Conclusion*).

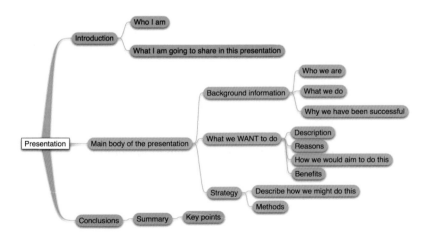

There are many mind mapping programs available for all platforms. NovaMind (*www.novamind.com*), available for both Windows and Mac, was used to draw these mind maps.

Use an Outliner Program

Outliners have been around for many years and remain popular tools for getting ideas together and creating order from the chaotic bits of information we collect when we start planning a presentation. These programs let you start with the highest level titles which help you plan the overall structure of the presentation before generating sublevels (Level 2, Level 3 and so on). At any time, the levels may be collapsed down so you only see the bits you want to see. For example, if you wanted to see only the titles of your slides you would tell the program to hide all the sublevels. When you want to see these again you simply expand the outliner so it shows all layers of your document.

Let's say we wanted our presentation to have 3 main sections:

1. Introduction

2. Main Presentation

3. Conclusion

We would generate these as our Level 1 headings.

Within Level 1 we might have a subheading listing the main subitems of the main presentation. Our second Level 1 heading would be "Main Presentation" and this would have several subheadings (Level 2) and each of these might have sub-subheadings (Level 3).

If you need to change the order of one of the subheadings it can be moved up and down until you find the place where it fits best. The beauty of the software is that the sub-subheadings attached to the headings follow the subheadings so everything is in the correct place.

There are numerous companies selling outliners but you might want to try Microsoft Word's outlining program first since this may be all you need.

Outliner software

There are many programs on the market including OmniOutliner and OmniGraffle. These all do pretty much the same thing and there is little to choose between them.

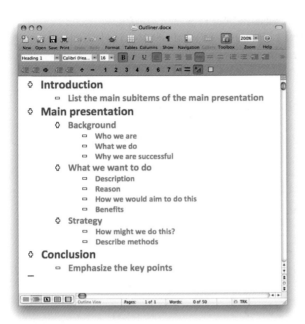

Outline of presentation in Microsoft Word showing 3 Levels.

The same document with outline collapsed showing only Level 1.

Tailoring Your Presentation

Beware

Write your presentation for the specific audience you are addressing. Never deliver a "generic" presentation.

I have said this before and will repeat it throughout the book: *Rule number one*: the audience comes first. It's a bit like being a shop-owner where the customer is king, you have been invited to give a presentation – not to bolster your ego. You are there to inform, entertain or sell to the audience. For this reason you owe it to them not to use bad material, poorly designed audiovisuals and incoherent text. This is about them, not you.

Avoid using "generic presentations" where you show the same slides or deliver the same pitch irrespective of who you are talking to. It does not work! Avoid the one-size-fits-all approach. It is lazy and unfair on the audience. The practice is pretty common nowadays, largely because we are all very busy and it is quicker to recycle an old talk than to write a fresh one.

You should aim to personalize your presentation for the intended audience.

Get this clear in your mind before you start
- What is the exact purpose of this presentation?
- What will the setting be?

  One-on-one?

  Small business meeting

  Informal briefing with larger audience?

  Formal presentation to a large audience?

- What have you been asked to do?

  Inform?

  Sell?

  Seek funding for a project?

- Who is the audience?

  The public?

  Junior professionals?

  Senior professionals?

- What do you think they want to get out of your presentation?

- How do you want them to react?

  Improve their understanding?

  Learn?

  Be entertained?

  Change behavior?

  Buy a product?

  Invest in your company?

- How should you pitch your talk?

  Chatty?

  Formal?

  Interactive?

Hot tip

If you have any doubt about the program or your role, ask the organizers.

Once you have a clear idea what it is you have been asked to cover, why and to whom, you can start designing your talk.

But

If you have any doubts concerning your remit and their expectations of you, ask the organizers early on and save yourself the embarrassment of delivering something they do not want or need.

Sourcing Material

So now you know what you need to present, and who the audience is you need to start constructing your presentation. What you need will depend on the type of presentation. For example, a five minute presentation to your own team providing a project update will require mainly text with little need for pictures. On the other hand, a formal speech to a medical audience about a specific disease and its treatment will need good graphics otherwise the talk will not hold their interest.

Hot tip

Use the Internet, books and journals for images, quotes and facts.

Information
This is key. You will want to share information and you will want the audience to *retain* some of what you say (the "Key Messages").

How to start gathering ideas
You are an expert in your field, and this is why you have been invited to talk. The best core knowledge is within your head. I would recommend starting with a blank notepad and suggest you jot down random thoughts concerning your talk. Think of items you may want to discuss. Think of the big picture – what is behind all this? What items help reinforce your message? If some seem less relevant, place these to one side for now. As you write down your ideas you will probably start to develop the theme for your presentation. It may be that you know the subject so well you can use your own ideas and thoughts alone and get to work on putting the talk together now. But often we need additional information from other sources.

Colleagues
Talk to colleagues in the same profession or office to see if they have any information related to your presentation. They may have review articles or possibly presentations on the same topic (but beware: *do not just reuse their old PowerPoint presentation!*).

Textbooks
Textbooks can be useful. For example if you are giving a college lecture to students, textbooks may be an invaluable resource. They may also provide images for your talk. Get yourself a good flatbed scanner and start collecting a store of images for your presentations (you cannot publish these since this would infringe copyright – and if you

show a scanned illustration you should always cite the source from which it was taken).

Journals

For academic talks journals are invaluable – they provide review articles and original research papers.

The Internet

There is a huge amount of information available on the web. Using a search engine you will find a ton of information. Be selective in what you read, print or use since the quality of the information varies.

Capture Internet content

Suppose you visit 20 websites and view 5 pages on each – you will have seen 100 pages overall. What do you do with all the information? Print it? This is very wasteful. Can it be captured? You can either switch on "off line browsing" in your browser or you can use software to store the content. For example Evernote (*www.evernote.com*) allows you to grab whole pages, images, PDFs and other content for viewing or printing later. You can create notebooks and subnotebooks so you can retrieve the information easily.

Hot tip

Buy a flatbed scanner – these are useful for grabbing images from books or journal articles.

Use Visuals!

Great text is very important in any presentation but without illustrations even the best talk could be boring. You need something to liven things up. If you look at the slides shown by the truly great presenters such as Guy Kawasaki (*www.truemors. com*), Steve Jobs (*www.apple.com*) and others you will see they often have one image on a slide with a couple of words. The one thing you will notice missing from their slides are bullet points!

Here is a simple slide I used to advertise a podcast which I had uploaded to iTunes. The slide is relatively sparse but contains enough information to let me talk about the podcast, how and why we made it.

Getting pictures
You can get royalty-free stock images online – but these are expensive, and you do not need 300 dots per inch (dpi) for PowerPoint – a lower resolution will project just as clearly.

Camera
Most people own digital cameras these days, so why not just take some pictures of your office, factory, staff, machines and drop these into PowerPoint? They will make your talk look more personal.

Internet
Maybe you need pictures of molecules or items which you cannot photograph easily? A useful source of pictures is the search engine Google (Google Images). You should see a clickable icon for Google Images if you go to *www.google.com*. Enter the word or phrase describing what you want. For example, if I wanted pictures of DNA molecules, I would type "DNA" and see what comes up:

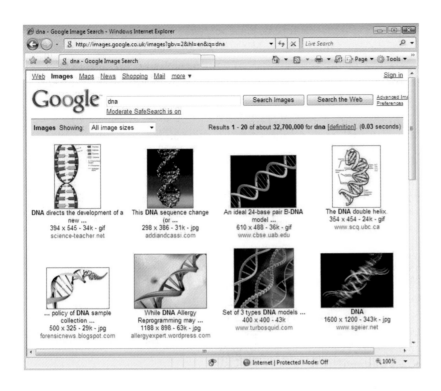

Don't forget

Keep track of your image files by using cataloging software on your PC.

To grab the image (make sure there are no copyright infringements) click on the thumbnail in the Google window and this will load the larger image. Just right-click the larger image and "**Save image as...**".

Scanners

Why not scan images from books or your company's brochures using a flatbed scanner? You only need to save at 75dpi unless you plan to print the image in which case you will need 300dpi.

Graphics from journal articles

Scientists often show graphics captured from papers published in journals. Often these are of poor quality and low resolution. One way to get high quality graphics from a journal article is to obtain the PDF file of the paper. Open this in Adobe Acrobat Reader or other PDF reader program. Find the graphic you want to capture and enlarge it on the screen so it fills your entire screen. At this point do a screen capture (**PrtScrn** or Snippet tool on Windows or **cmd + shift + 4** with a Mac). The image you have taken can be dropped into PowerPoint and will look stunning.

Less is More

This saying is absolutely true in the world of presentations. Many of us do not follow this rule, and because we are so keen to share our knowledge with the audience we include everything on the slides, making it virtually impossible to see the wood for the trees.

Re-focus on your key points. Write these on a card and keep this in front of you. As you go through the process of refining your material for the presentation ask yourself: *"Does this fit with my key messages?"* If not, discard.

Beware

Your slides are there to complement your speech and are not intended to be the speech.

Your slides should complement your speech but your slides should not *be* your speech. The words and images are really meant to reinforce the message as you go through your presentation. Although difficult, especially for beginners, you have to resist the temptation of putting all your words, data and pictures in the talk. Why not? The audience will read the slides. They always do and you can't stop them. The more words you have the more text they have to read. The more they read the less they listen to you.

Reducing the number of slides

For a 30 minute talk you will need around 30 slides, give or take a few. When we write a presentation we often end up with double that number. You probably feel all the information is essential but you need to get the slide number down somehow. Where there are graphs or other data, perhaps these can be combined on one slide.

Practice Makes Perfect

The best presenters make the whole process seem so natural. It is hard to imagine them having to rehearse a presentation. But the reason their presentations are so slick, moving seemlessly from slide to slide, is because they have spent *huge* amounts of time working on their story, rehearsing the flow through the entire presentation. If you want your presentation to have the *wow* factor you should invest time going through your talk several times before you give the actual presentation.

Keep a printed copy of your slides in your briefcase and read this during lunch, on the train, and on your way to the venue on the day. Or make a copy for your cell phone or PDA and review the slides there.

Hot tip

Rehearsal is essential and you cannot over-rehearse.

Benefits of rehearsal

- Helps you gauge time. You may have the right number of slides in the deck, but if you practice your talk you may find there are too many and your presentation will be rushed

- It helps you learn your material. You will have total mastery of the content if you go through it several times

- You will be less reliant on notes – you will know the material so well you will have little need for notes

Rehearsal methods

- Print off your handout and go through each slide saying out loud what you will say on the day (but do not memorize a speech!)

- Alternatively, load it onto the laptop and imagine you are giving the presentation for real

- Try to moderate your speed. When practicing we tend to rush through the presentation. On the big day you may find you are running out of time because you are going slower since you have to explain charts or diagrams

- Try to record yourself – either audio or video

- Practice 6, or 12 times so there are no slides, pictures or words that surprise you

- Is there any section you stumble over? If so, go over that bit until it feels right and you know what to say

Summary

- Adequate preparation is essential if you want to make an impact

- Write down your key messages. Keep these near you so you can stay focused as you write your talk and design your slides

- Avoid using the computer *initially* – it is better to start with paper and pencil

- Jot down all your ideas on paper then try an outlining or mind mapping program to organize these threads

- Do not worry about the relevance of all the things you write down – most will be discarded later

- Use the outliner or mind mapper to help you construct your slides

- You must tailor each presentation for the specific audience you are addressing. Make sure you are clear about who they are, what they know, what they want to know

- Avoid reusing old slides but you can recycle the graphics if they are of good quality

- Material for presentation should be primarily generated by you since you are knowledgeable in the area in which you are presenting. You can later supplement your outline with information obtained from the media, journals, textbooks, the Internet and colleagues

- Graphics add interest to slides and also allow you to keep the text content of the slides low

- Use good quality images (photographs if possible) and avoid using animations or clip art since these are often of poor quality and of doubtful value in your presentation

- Rehearse as many times as you can. The more times you go through your slides the more control you will have. The information and slides will be second nature and totally ingrained. Avoid learning a speech but work out well ahead of time what you will say (approximately) when each slide is shown

4 Raising The Bar

Most presentations are boring because the standard is set pretty low and little thought goes into design of the slides. In this section we examine ways of improving slides and dealing with bad habits.

Death by PowerPoint

Beware

PowerPoint and similar programs are great presentation tools but can be boring.

Millions of presentations are given daily but most of them are second or third rate at best. They are boring, ill-thought out and delivered by presenters who appear indifferent to the material they are presenting. They seem to lack the passion and drive we associate with really great presenters. This is a real shame, because people have to sit and listen to these tedious monologs.

As we have already discussed, effective presentations should have focus, significance, be fairly "simple" in design terms, and should convey key messages that are remembered by the audience. And don't forget, being a good presenter can enhance your career enormously.

The role models we see presenting well (TV presenters, Seth Godin, Guy Kawasaki, Steve Jobs, Garr Reynolds and others) inspire the audiences. Their messages are crystal clear, their graphics and text fit the speech perfectly and we can recall much of what we hear. Yet, in reality, when it comes to presenting at work, we emulate our peers using the same clichéd PowerPoint templates, poor quality graphics and bullet points galore. Maybe this is an exaggeration but it is not far off the truth!

Net result
Most presentations are *very boring*.

Rules are meant to be broken
There is no reason why you should have to stick to "convention" and there are lots of ways you can spruce up your presentations to make them look stunning. These will be covered later in the book but consider ways your performances could be improved. What would enhance your presentations and make them memorable?

1. **Focus:** The content must be crystal clear

2. **Content:** Should be well written with no ambiguity. The text should be minimal since the purpose is to provide an anchor so the audience knows where they are. The text is not meant to deliver the entire speech

3. **Use the correct number of slides:** There is no correct number. Some very experienced presenters can captivate an audience for an hour using only a few slides.

Others can use 80 or more and yet the audience does not feel overloaded because the slides contain mainly images rather than bulleted text lists. As a rule of thumb, it is safer to use about 1 slide per minute of your allotted time

4 **Avoid templates:** If you must use PowerPoint (standard in the business world today) or Keynote slide programs, avoid most of the templates. They are contrived and distracting, full of embellishments that do nothing for your presentation. It is safer to stick to a plain background. We will discuss slide design later in the book

5 **Graphics:** Invest some time locating good quality graphics for your talks and remove any cheap clip art from your slides

Beware

Templates save time but often have distracting backgrounds and unnecessary effects.

Here is one of my own slides before and after tidying up and slimming down the text a little.

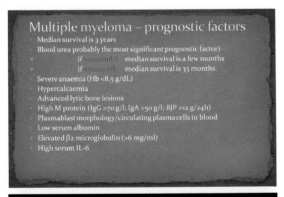

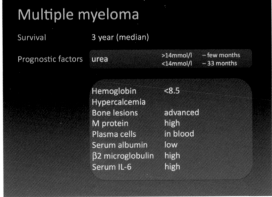

Deliver With Passion

It should go without saying that passion, enthusiasm and drive can only enhance your presentations. These are what bring your talk to life. Of course we will all continue to use PowerPoint, but without infectious enthusiasm, even the most spectacular slideshows may be dull if the presenter lacks enthusiasm.

Can this be learned?

Being a great presenter requires a degree of confidence. This will come with practice – the more talks you give, the better you will feel about giving talks, and the process builds incrementally.

Knowing your subject helps as well. When presenting a talk which deals with unfamiliar content it is very difficult to be persuasive since you are not really an authority in the area. Some of the things you say may be incorrect and the Question and Answer session at the end may prove challenging!

I have seen people give talks for others. For example, at international medical conferences there are sometimes clashes in the timetables where a speaker is due to be in two places at the same time. Rather than decline an invitation to present their data they will ask a colleague to give their talk. I have never had to delegate for someone in this situation but I cannot imagine it being a very powerful or persuasive presentation.

Ownership

To present well you need to "own" the material. It has to contain your ideas, thoughts, text, images and synthesis. The key messages are what you want the audience to remember. You don't care if they cannot recall the main text of your speech – so long as they remember the essential key messages!

Be more caring

You have to care about what you do. You should always put the audience's needs before yours. As we have seen, this is about *them*, not you. You must have pride in your work and efforts putting the presentation together. You need to appear to enjoy the opportunity to present to them (this is much more difficult than it sounds and we will discuss ways of appearing at ease even when you are terrified, later).

Accept criticism

No-one will write and deliver the perfect presentation first time. People underestimate how long it will take to write a good presentation. Putting together a knock-out speech takes a great deal of time and effort. Even if you are only going to present for 15 minutes you will need to invest many hours putting this together if you want it to be a truly memorable experience for the audience.

Don't forget

Accept criticism – it will ultimately help you deliver better presentations.

63

Rehearse, rehearse and rehearse some more!

You have put in the time, researched the field well and have written the presentation. But you are only halfway there since rehearsal is the bedrock of a good speech. You should aim to go through your speech many times, altering text on your slides and working out what you will say and the order in which you will say it. You should rehearse using a laptop or desktop computer, using the rehearsal tools in PowerPoint or whichever software you intend to use. This will give you a rough idea how long it will take to present your slides. Bear in mind that we tend to run through our slides faster when we rehearse.

Tricks of The Trade

The first 2 minutes

This is the golden period where the mold is set for your presentation. If you have a strong start, thanking the organizers and introducing yourself to the audience then the rest of the talk will likely flow well. However, if you have a fumbling start, with a rambling introduction then it is quite difficult to recover. Unfortunately, the first couple of minutes are when you are at your most nervous and you need to concentrate especially hard on the opening moments in order to get you off to a head start. Never *ever* begin by saying "*Can everyone hear me okay?*" – this sounds very amateur and must be avoided at all costs!

Nerves and stagefright

Presenting is stressful and, even when armed with a great presentation, some people will lose it and fall apart, expressing themselves badly, playing with coins in their pocket or with their hair. The trick here is to try to look relaxed, calm and in control. Chapter 7 deals with techniques that will help you remain poised throughout your presentation

Good material

Having a good story with appropriate graphics will help boost your confidence – make sure the key messages are crisp and memorable!

Positioning

Standing behind the podium feels safe. We can grab the sides and we are unassailable, almost. But this is like presenting from behind a screen and the podium or lectern effectively becomes a barrier between you and the audience. Since your main aim is to engage the audience it seems crazy to put obstacles in the way. Sadly, many conferences are rather old-fashioned and all the speakers have to stand on the same spot because there is no lapel microphone and you cannot venture away from the podium.

Facial expressions

You may not feel much like smiling but try to smile as you approach the podium or stage and start to address the audience. It gives them the impression that you are relaxed even if you do not feel relaxed. This gives you the confidence to *be* relaxed and perform at your best.

Look them in the eye!

It is irritating to listen to a presenter who does not engage the audience. It does not matter how well you articulate the words or how good your slides are, if you fail to make eye contact with the faces in the audience you will be marked down. It is not easy looking at everyone but try to scan from side to side so that the entire group feels as though you are talking to them.

Don't forget

Look the audience in the eye and get them engaged.

Don't slouch

Stand up straight, look composed and avoid huddling over the laptop.

Speak slowly

Human nature being what it is, we tend to speak more quickly when we are nervous. Consciously try to slow your speech down. Imagine almost that you are talking to someone who does not understand English very well.

Hands

Where do you put them? In your pockets? Absolutely not. Clasped in front of you? Again, probably not. Move your hands to drive the points home and to help you connect with your audience. Watch politicians – they use their hands very expressively but not intrusively. When you next attend a good presentation, watch the presenter's mannerisms and in particular his or her body language, including the hands.

65

Banish Bad Habits

Playing with your hair or with coins in your pockets is off-putting so you need to watch for any repetitive bad habits you may have. It is worth making a video of yourself giving a presentation to see what you look like. You will spot your bad habits much more easily that way! Try not to "*um*" and "*er*" as you present. It is very irritating to the listener. If you find yourself doing this, make a conscious effort to stop. It can be corrected fairly easily.

Beware

Poor laser control irritates the audience.

Laser pointer
This is a useful aid to help you point out specific items on a slide but don't overuse it. Some presenters highlight almost every word using the laser pointer and it becomes like a karaoke show where you have to watch the bouncing ball move along the words on the slide.

Microphone
If you have one it will help the whole room to hear what you say. Lapel mikes are useful since you can move around the room. Fixed mikes on the lectern require you to face the microphone and speak a few inches away from it. When presenters look at their slides and turn their heads their voices go quiet then loud then quiet and this can be irritating for the audience.

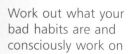

Hot tip

Work out what your bad habits are and consciously work on these.

Don't read your slides
The main reason for using slides in a presentation is to provide some form of reinforcement for the audience. The slide should complement what you are saying and should not be a verbatim account of what you intend to say. Keep slides simple and complementary.

Control your speed
Anxiety and the adrenaline rush leads to speech which is much faster than normal. This generally leads to a presentation which may be difficult for the audience to follow, as you proceed at high speed through your slides. Try to learn to moderate your speed and consciously speak *slower* than you normally would.

Complex graphics
Too many presentations have horrendously complicated figures which take the presenter ages to explain. It may be that presenters feel that if the slides are very complex they will look more impressive, but the opposite is true.

How to end your presentation

Just as the first few minutes are important in order to boost your confidence, many people find the closing statement tricky. By the time you have delivered your presentation you will be keen to get off the stage and out of the limelight.

Avoid

Saying *"Well, that's about it..."*. Alternatively some speakers just stop talking and look out at the audience who are unsure what to do. Has the speaker finished? Is he just pausing? Can we applaud now?

Do

Say something like *"It has been a real pleasure talking to you today, thank you for your attention."*, or even just *"Thank you for your attention"*. This last phrase is the one most commonly used in the scientific and medical communities. Whatever you use, make it very obvious that you have finished and the audience will applaud! They need a verbal cue from you to say *"OK, now I have finished and you can start asking questions"*.

Handing Q & A Sessions

This can be more tricky than the presentation itself. At this stage you may feel vulnerable since you do not know what questions will be asked. Remember – you know more than they do about this topic. Also bear in mind that they are not trying to trick you but genuinely want to ask questions and learn from you. We will cover this in Chapter 10.

Hot tip

Learn how to end your presentation gracefully.

67

Seek Feedback

Why bother with feedback?

You may think you are fantastic (and maybe you are) but as we know it's not about you! The audience may think differently. And don't just ask a colleague in the audience *"Was that okay?"* – what else can they say but *"Sure, it was great!"*

Providing feedback is a very powerful learning tool. At the same time it can be destructive, since people are often fragile and find it difficult to accept criticism.

Be careful how you provide feedback to a speaker. Keep your comments as specific as possible, don't just say *"It was great"* or *"You didn't perform well today"*. Instead, let them know which parts were good, and which did not work.

Try to provide positive feedback before negative – this softens the blow and is far less destructive than the other way round.

Hot tip

Actively seek feedback. It helps you improve your delivery.

If you are seeking feedback following your own presentation ask people:

- What they liked

- What they did not like, and why

Ask them about

- Content

- Delivery

- Your use of graphics and other visuals

Feedback forms

Often, especially for meetings with educational content, there will be a feedback form which rates the speakers on whether the talk delivered what the audience expected, the speaker's style, and other factors. Reading these can be like receiving your school report. They often make us feel annoyed but generally the audience is correct, so do not disregard their comments.

The audience will pick up on things like lack of clarity, having too many slides or speakers who rush through their material (trying to pack as much as possible into your session is very common). Try to take notice of what they say and modify your next presentation bearing the feedback in mind.

Don't forget

Review the feedback forms even if they are critical. What areas do you need to work on?

Universities and colleges

These institutions use peer observation of teaching, where a lecturer will sit in on one lecture given by a colleague. He or she will then complete an evaluation form and submit this to the university.

The business world

Your skills as a speaker may be part of your appraisal and any shortcomings may be highlighted when you sit down with your manager. If there is one area where you are weak this is worth discussing. Maybe they run internal courses which teach this skill?

Design Does Matter

Maybe you are stuck in a rut and looking for ways to improve your presenting style? You can try the techniques in this book which will help, but you might also try some of the more abstract concepts listed here.

Beware

Slides are not just gratuitous wallpaper – getting the design and content right matters.

Ban blue backgrounds

People have been using PowerPoint with blue backgrounds and white text you many years. Part of the reason is because it is easy to see in the dark room of a conference. The reason this still has become *de rigueur* is because long ago, before people made their own slides using PowerPoint, you had

to type out your text onto sheets of paper, using a typewriter. This was then photographed onto 35mm film by an illustration department who would then apply a blue background leaving the text white. Once computers came along we tried to emulate this – hence the blue background became the standard for presentations.

You could use other colors or even go with white, although very light colors are better for small group meetings in a lit room. You could try a black background or dark gray, perhaps. Just be careful when using templates – they tend to be over-embellished.

What's wrong with this slide?

> ### CLINICAL GOVERNANCE
> ### BACKGROUND:-
>
> - 'The new NHS: Modern, Dependable' and
>   'A First Class Service: Quality in the new NHS'
>   - place a duty of clinical governance on health authorities, PCGs and Trusts.
> - Objectives reflected in the Health Improvement Programme (HImP).
> - The HA will hold Trusts, Primary Care and 3rd party providers accountable.
> - Trusts will need a system backed by a statutory duty for quality.
> - Two new central bodies will be set up with a remit for CG - 'NICE' and 'CHImp'.
> - Existing national inspectorates, colleges and specialist societies will continue to have a key role.
> - National Service Frameworks outlining 'good practice' will be developed.
>   - Cancer (Calman-Hine), Cardiovascular disease and Mental Health.
> - Clinical outcomes will be measured using centrally driven directives
>   -'Our Healthier Nation', league tables and the Performance Assessment Framework.

Apart from being blue with white writing there are several sins on this slide (which happens to be my colleague's slide!) For example, the font is Times New Roman which is great for *The Times* newspaper but not the best font for presentations. The slide is designed like a document rather than a visual aid! There is too much text. It has more bullets than a Western and there is even underlining (*who underlines nowadays?*) and a strange punctuation mark ":-" which secretaries in the 1920s probably used!

Lose the bullets

Why not try making your slides but switch off the bullets. This is more difficult than it sounds since the use of bullets is so widespread it is second nature to most of us. After you remove bullets, start taking out words or even whole lines of text. Slim the content down to the bare minimum.

Find examples of good design

Look at signs, magazines, TV ads and see if there are any ideas you can use in your slides. Advertising companies demand huge fees because they are very skilled at selling through the use of stunning graphics and clever fonts. Don't go crazy with the fonts, though, since you may find that your font is not installed on the computer you are using at the venue and everything will default to something like Arial and look awful!

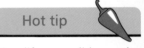

Hot tip

Simplify your slides and avoid bullet points if you can.

Old Habits

One Message

One Story

Sourcing Images

Most presenters, even some fairly senior managers, think little about the images in their presentations. Many use none at all, preferring to design slides that are wall-to-wall text. As a spectator this is pretty boring.

It is very useful to have pictures, graphs, diagrams, photomicrographs or even abstract design to help lift the monotony of presentations.

There are various options available to you and we'll start with the basic "artwork" that most people drop onto their slides: clip art.

Clip art

These are line drawings, or other artwork, often supplied by program manufacturers. You will find them in a folder on your PC or Mac and they can be accessed from within the program you are running, such as Microsoft Word, or PowerPoint.

The artwork is pretty clichéd now, and you will see lots of people use the same illustrations. The problem is that if I saw this in a 7 year old's presentation I might think it is cute but in a serious presentation at a conference I think it's fairly unforgivable. Solution? Avoid at all cost. Do *not* use free clip art.

Photo libraries on disk or from the web

There are several software houses that supply good quality photographs that are royalty-free. You can even publish these in books (but check the small print on the CD cover). Have a look in your local computer store in the "Computer Art" section and you will probably find a selection. You can also buy images from iStockphoto, Shutterstock and others but this a fairly expensive option.

Here are two examples from a low cost CD set (the CD contains 150,000 photographs).

Hot tip

Use images to break up text. Take pictures using a digital camera or use the web to source them.

Use slideshare

Join slideshare (*www.slideshare.net*) and download (and upload) slides. Look at the slides on offer critically. What do you like? What do you not like, and why? Does this help with your own slides?

Become a photographer

Start taking photos. Use a good camera and change your settings to "ultra-fine" (or whatever your camera uses for its high resolution images if you plan to publish the images). Take photographs of buildings, items, your workplace, machines, or whatever you fancy  (providing there are no photography restrictions, of course). Some of these may be great material for your slides.

Start a photo library

Keep your photographs cataloged on your PC or Mac. Use software such as Adobe Lightroom, Microsoft Expression Media, Extensis Portfolio, or iPhoto to store your images. Ask your colleagues if they have any they wish to add to the scheme.

What format for pictures?

Generally we use settings on our cameras such as "ultra-fine" for photos of family, friends and landscapes. These high resolution images are great for printing since there will be no pixellation of the image. For presentation slides save images as JPEGs or TIFFs.

But, if you were to use these in a slideshow

- The file would become bloated and enormous

- When projecting them on a screen through an AV projector no-one would know how detailed they are because the projectors can only display at lower resolutions. So save space in your PowerPoint file by using 75dpi images

Learn to use drawing software

Line art, flow diagrams, and the like are useful but learn how to use the software and avoid over-colored poor quality drawings. Adobe Illustrator is the industry standard but is expensive. Look for cheaper shareware vector or line drawing software.

Beware

You do not need to store your images as high resolution files – 75dpi is fine for projection.

Hot tip

Don't aim for average – with some effort you can be outstanding.

Final Thoughts

Don't aim for average
You have seen *average* enough times. Do your utmost not to be in that group.

Be intimate
Work with the audience, bond with them and develop a conversation with them rather than lecture *at* them. Present to the whole room and not just a couple of faces. Create intimacy. Invite discussion during your presentation – this prevents it being a monolog.

Invest time in creating your presentation
A long presentation takes a substantial amount of time to prepare. A short presentation takes even longer. Be committed to put the time in and perfect your presentation.

Can you condense your talk?
Could you condense your presentation into one single point? Could you at least convert it into the "elevator pitch" where your entire message could be conveyed in a couple of minutes? Try it!

Go through your slides and reduce the content as much as you possibly can while still retaining its meaning.

Remove the sub-bullets – they shouldn't be there.

Then remove the bullets (most people find this very difficult).

Rehearse
Rehearse your presentation so you know it by heart. You should know what you are going to say for each slide in your presentation. However, do not memorize your speech – you will sound wooden and inflexible.

Focus
Focus on what you want to say. Don't let the slides put you off. They should not be a straightjacket – they are there to support you, not constrain you. Try glancing at the screen when you change slide but do not focus on the words or read the words.

Blank slides
Try inserting blank slides at places where you want to discuss points or make the audience reflect on points you have covered previously. You may feel exposed and vulnerable since your script has disappeared but if used well it can be very dramatic.

Stop talking

After you have made an important point, rather than just move on to the next slide, pause for 10 or 20 seconds. Like the blank slide this may feel odd and you will worry that the audience thinks you have forgotten your lines! But this is a powerful technique used by great presenters.

What to write first – slides or speech

It is probably best to design the slides then work out what speech goes best with these.

Technology

A technically brilliant presentation can still flop. Do not be mesmerized by animations or moving backgrounds. These are bling and add nothing to your talk. The best talks are very simple designs with incredibly powerful messages.

Sit or stand?

Sometimes in smaller business meetings people sit down to present. In general it is better to stand if you are presenting to more than 3 or 4 people.

No jokes!

Telling jokes is risky but you can be humorous.

Remove sub-bullets

Remove bullets

Remove unnecessary words & phrases

Leave the bare minimum

Summary

- PowerPoint and other slide programs can make below average presentations acceptable. But do not be swayed by the glitz of templates and animations. Keep your slides simple

- Retain your focus at all times, focussing on both the content and the audience. The show is not about you

- Deliver your presentations with passion. Learn to exude confidence and your presentations will hit home effectively

- Aim to sweep the audience off their feet

- Expect and learn to accept constructive criticism. This will help you iron out problems and will make you a better presenter

- Rehearse constantly – know your subject matter inside out. Do not memorize your slides but know what is on each and every one of them, and be very clear in your mind what you are going to say when each slide appears

- Slides complement your speech but they are not, in themselves, the content of your speech

- The first 2 minutes are crucial for an effective presentation. Spend time concentrating on your opening statement. This will help boost your confidence when it goes well

- Speak more slowly than you normally would and use your hands for emphasis. Do not keep your hands in your pockets or play with items at the lectern

- Survey the entire audience, engage them and talk to them all

- Work out what your bad habits are and control these

- If necessary video yourself giving a talk and watch this so you can see if you have any tics or unwanted mannerisms

- Design does matter – spend time on slide design and obtain high quality graphics

- Avoid making jokes during your presentation – these seldom work and are too risky. Humor, however, is useful for breaking the ice and making both you and the audience relax

5 Different Audiences

You may be great at presenting to large audiences yet fail to get your messages across to an individual or small group. You need to be flexible and tailor your approach to suit the situation.

Presenting One-on-One

This is a more intimate form of presentation, where you are presenting to an individual. You may be trying to sell, persuade or inform.

Dress

It is best to dress smartly with a suit and tie for men, or business attire for women. Chinos and open necked shirt will look odd if the person you are presenting to is smartly dressed and you will lose any authority you might otherwise have had, unless you are a student meeting your supervisor.

Body language and mannerisms become even more important in small group presentations. Don't forget to smile!

Timing

Get there early. Poor time-keeping may blow the whole thing. When shown into the room, you must aim to appear confident. Walk towards the person you will be addressing and shake hands. Sit when asked. Hopefully there will be a desk where you can set up your laptop or put your papers (*remember to ask first*). Avoid sitting too close – personal space invasion will ruin your pitch.

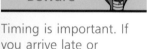

Beware

Timing is important. If you arrive late or overrun you will be marked down.

This style of meeting is suitable for:

- Selling something

- Seeking financial support

- Mentoring or appraising a colleague

- Updating a senior colleague on a research project or activity

Preparation

Do some homework and learn about the company, what it does, what it needs, and how it operates. Obtain this information on the Internet or from company brochures.

Introductions

Tell them exactly who you are, why you are here and in what capacity. You can give them the key message(s) now since this will help create a strong opening and get them interested.

Opening

Just as with a standard presentation the opening moments are important. You must make a good impression. If you fail to do so, it will be very difficult to recover. Around 80% of sales are estimated to be down to the strength of the opening statement.

Try to work out what their company needs. Tell them something they don't know (rather than all the things they *do* know). The person you are presenting to will decide very quickly whether they like you or not. You will only have a fixed amount of time to make your pitch so use it well and keep to time.

Main body of presentation

After the opening moments, proceed through your presentation for 15 minutes or however long you have. Conclude and allow plenty of time for them to ask questions. You may also wish to question them about specific points about the company. If they are still interested they will usually be happy to answer these.

What can go wrong?

Anxiety can adversely affect even a one-on-one presentation and things that can go wrong include:

- Not keeping to time. Overrunning is a cardinal sin and will reflect very badly on your performance overall. Factor in time for interjections which can throw your timing out

- Talking too much. Let them do some talking! It's not about you!

- Being over-critical of competitors

- Lack of flexibility. You cannot be deflected from your pitch and you are determined to say all you want to say in a very specific order. Learn to be more flexible

- Forgetting to actually *present*. You are *not* there for a chat – your role is to present on behalf of your company

- Prolonged eye contact. Do not stare. In some cultures (Asia, for example) staring is regarded as rude so avoid it. Even in the US and Europe it is not a good idea to stare

Remain composed, sit upright and don't relax in the chair even if you feel relaxed.

Answer questions professionally, thank him or her for their time and leave confidently, then exit gracefully.

 Beware

Do not talk too much and remember to get your key messages across.

Presenting a Business Plan

Perhaps you might be trying to secure funding for a project or business venture. This is a form of sales presentation, so similar rules apply.

Getting investment is not easy so you will need to be very passionate about the proposal and enthusiastic in your presentation. Be as personable as you can without being overbearing.

If there are several people in the room, make sure you address each one of them and make eye contact with each of them regularly. Try to avoid talking only to the person who seems most benign since this will alienate the others and you need them *all* to be on your side.

Preparation
Prepare well. Do your homework, learn about the investors and ensure you have *all* your facts and figures in your head. Dress smartly.

How much time do you have available?
The golden rule applies: do not overrun your time. These people are short of time and may only give you 20 minutes or less. Make the most of it.

Body of the presentation
As always, you need a good structure:

- Overview of the proposal

- Staff – let them know who is working on it or who you would hire if you had the funding, and what their roles would be

- Purpose of the product – is there an unmet need?

- Detailed financial accounts

    Revenue

    Turnover in the last year

Profit

Predicted profit next year, and the year after

Expenses

● Current investors

Who are they ?

How much have they invested?

You may need to bring letters or evidence of investment

● The market

Have you done market research? If not, why not?

Why now?

Why do you think it will succeed?

● Competition

● Patent rights

● What is your overall strategy?

● Potential partners

● Funding

How much do you want?

What you would do with the funding if it were available?

● What's in it for them? Make it sound as attractive as possible

After the pitch you will receive a barrage of questions. Be prepared. If you look blankly, especially when asked a basic question, you will not be in the room very long. Be polite. Keep calm and composed. You may consult notes providing it does not take you 10 minutes to find the relevant facts. However, if you do not know an answer *say so* – do not make things up. Honesty is regarded as a positive.

Small Group Discussion

This could be a tutorial group, a team briefing, sales pitch to a number of people from a company, or any small meeting with between 6 and 12 people.

The setting
A circular table is best if you can find one. If not, use a regular one. If you want to dominate the meeting sit at the head of a rectangular table but if you want equality with the others a round table is best.

Structure of the presentation
- Why are we here?

- Lead them through the main content of your presentation

- Conclude

How much to say?
This depends on why you are there:

- Selling

- Presenting data or finances

- Teaching

- Exploring

- Research meeting

Do you have an agenda you intend to follow?

Prepare this in advance and bring sufficient copies to hand round. It is better to email these in advance if possible. Lead them through the agenda. Make it as interactive as possible and get the group involved.

Be aware:

- Dynamics – politics and personalities become much more obvious in a small group meeting than during a standard lecture. Some participants may dislike other members of the group. Sometimes individuals feel intimidated by others. Some will talk and others will remain silent. You need to mediate and facilitate so that everyone is heard.

- Dominant participants – you may find these difficult to control but you can use tactics like saying "*That's great, but I wonder if we could get some input from ...*" or "*There are one or two people we haven't heard from yet...*".

Beware

Domineering individuals may hijack the meeting – try to learn how to control these.

Outcomes

This depends on the purpose of the meeting. If you are the "leader" try to wrap things up and recap briefly on what was discussed. If there are actions from the meeting, you might want to remind the participants of what is expected of them before the next meeting. Send an email thanking the participants.

Chairing a Meeting

This is a key skill and one that is often underestimated. We have all attended meetings where there is a chairman. Sometimes we are critical of the chair saying he or she did not control the meeting well, allowed the agenda to be hijacked, and so on. However, until you have chaired a meeting yourself, you do not realize how complicated and stressful the chairing process is! A good chair can ensure a meeting goes smoothly and to time, with a consensus reached. A bad chair will have the opposite result.

Role of the chair

- To be an impartial facilitator

- Makes sure the meeting achieves its intended aims

- Follows the agenda

- Makes sure everyone is heard

- Keeps to time

A good chair should:

- Organize in advance

- Have a good working knowledge of the topics on the agenda

- Have a clear written agenda sent out well in advance, along with any relevant papers

- Know the committee members

- Be assertive but not domineering. He or she must be able to stand his or her ground

- Keep everything on track

- Summarize the meeting points – use this to wind up topics (avoids prolonged discussion where consensus not reached)

- Give everyone an overview of what was discussed and the action points agreed

- Be tactful

- Work closely with the meeting secretary to agree the agenda and review the minutes of the meeting

- Finish on time

Running the meeting

- The chair should introduce him or herself

- Welcome new members

- Go round the table inviting the members to introduce themselves if there are new members present

- The chair can use slides, overheads or flip-charts as necessary

- Can invite outside speakers to present for specific items

The chair should avoid

- Dominating the meeting, talking too much

- Trying to cover too much detail

- Overrunning

- Taking sides in arguments

- Forcing his or her ideas on the group

Beware

As chair, avoid forcing your opinions on the group. Stay neutral.

Hot tip

Pay attention to the rules the organizers provide – this may save embarrassment later.

Academic Conferences

These events are often attended by very large numbers of delegates. Conference presentations are generally subdivided into several types of talk:

- Plenary sessions

- Guest lectures

- Simultaneous free communications

- Breakfast expert meetings

These affairs tend to be fairly rigid. Instructions are generally sent out well ahead of the meeting. Talks have clearly defined time limits (often 10 minutes with 5 minutes for questions). They will usually provide all the AV equipment and expect you to bring your  presentation on a memory stick or CD-ROM. The organizers may request that you email your presentation some days before the conference. They will usually only accept PowerPoint slides, rather than Keynote or other formats. For logistical reasons they will not allow presenters to use their own laptops.

Dress

This varies. Many people present wearing smart-casual attire. Others prefer business suits. Wear what you think will fit best. Check the instructions you have received to see whether this gives any clue as to what to wear. If you really have no idea, then dress fairly smartly since it is better to be a little over-dressed than under-dressed.

Presentation structure

This will follow the usual *Introduction*, *Body* and *Conclusion*. Because time is tight, for a standard 15 minute presentation you should only use about 12 or 15 slides. Your introduction will need to be very brief with most of the time allocated to the body of the talk which will contain your data and interpretation.

Your conclusion slide will need to be strong, and will usually summarize the key points from the body with your main scientific conclusions.

Interaction

These events are usually not interactive. There will be no questions during your presentation Instead, these are kept for the 5 minute slot right at the end. If you overrun your presentation you will eat into the short question time and this will be viewed dimly by the audience.

Plenary talks usually have no questions. They are just didactic lectures, often for 45 minutes or more after which the audience applauds then the speaker leaves the podium.

Overrunning

Do not overrun. You will lose valuable question time or, even worse, you will encroach on to the next speaker's time which is viewed as bad practice. It indicates poor planning.

Rehearsal

Since time is so tight, and because you are presenting to a large group of (usually very knowledgeable) individuals you need to rehearse rigorously for this type of event. More than ever, you need to know exactly what to say for every slide that you show. If you have complex graphics or diagrams, factor in the time needed to explain these.

International Meetings

The most common setting is probably the international specialist conference. Many organizations in science and medicine host meetings abroad. You may be invited to give a state-of-the-art lecture or perhaps a free communication. Either way, the advice is the same.

English is usually the preferred language. Most papers and communications are written in English.

Preparation
You need to prepare your presentation as you would for any presentation – with a clear structure and memorable key points. Find out how long the talk is expected to last and how many minutes you will have for questions. Your speed of delivery will need to be considerably *slower* than for a native English-speaking audience. Use less slides otherwise you risk overrunning your slot.

Delivery
Speak slowly and try to pause frequently to make sure the audience has taken in what you have just said. Don't rush from slide to slide since you will lose them early on and they may never catch up.

DO
- Speak slowly and deliberately

- Be aware of local culture e.g. clothing requirements for women (Islamic and some Asian cultures)

- If you are meeting businessmen make sure you know how to greet them, and shake hands

- In Japan and some other countries you may have to bow – ask the person organizing the meeting how this is done

- In business, the exchange of business cards is expected. In

Beware

Don't overuse jargon, colloquialisms or talk too quickly or you risk losing an international audience.

the West, we tend to simply hand these out to people who often put them in their top jacket pocket with hardly a glance. In many cultures you will be handed a business card face up, using both hands to pass the card. You are expected to read the card carefully before placing it in your own business card holder

- It is always best to check out the web for advice concerning local culture and customs – for example *www.cyborlink.com*

- Be aware of colors and their use in presentations. White is great for the US or Europe since it is associated with simplicity or purity but in Asian cultures it is associated with death. Red in China means happiness but in Western cultures it is often used for anger!

- If you are invited to eat a meal with your colleagues in that country you must try your best to eat, otherwise this will be taken as a signal of rejection

- Watch your body language – especially since many gestures and stances may be construed as threatening or impolite

DON'T

- Use colloquialisms and abbreviations – these will be largely meaningless in that culture

- Use acronyms – always say the full name

- Use humor – it often fails with English-speaking audiences so it is not going to work where English is not the first language

- Use prolonged eye contact especially when close up – in many Asian and Islamic cultures this is seen as rudeness

- Use graphics that might offend. For example, a thumbs up photo would be associated as "well done!" or "good job!" in the US or Europe but it does not mean the same in all cultures

- Dress inappropriately – for men it is best to wear a suit and tie. For women it might be advisable to wear a head scarf and cover the arms

Hot tip

Research the culture of the country you are visiting. The Internet is a useful place to start.

Chairing a Conference

Acting as chair for a conference is more stressful than giving a presentation. You need to help plan the program, introduce the speakers, get the audience excited about the content, keep the speakers to time, and help with the Q & A session.

Program planning

Contact your speakers before the meeting and discuss titles for their presentations, and help them plan the content of their talks.

Research the speakers

You will need to introduce them to the audience so find out something about each speaker. Ask them to provide biosketches, and check their company or university website for information. If they are widely published, find out what their major contributions have been. Build them up, but try not to go overboard.

Warm up the crowd

As the host you will need to open the meeting, thanking all the attendees for coming. Provide an overview of the meeting. Get them excited about the talks they are about to hear. Develop the theme of the session in order to put the speakers' presentations in context.

Introductions

Introduce each speaker using notes you have made. Write down key points on index cards, one for each speaker. Provide a glimpse of what the speaker will be discussing. Avoid reading your notes and make your style as conversational as possible. Invite the speaker onto the stage and begin the applause (the audience will follow your lead).

Keep speakers to time

When the speaker has used up the allotted time, you could move towards the podium, perhaps sitting at the desk on the stage. This alerts the speaker that his or her time has been used up.

Question session

Your role is to invite questions, asking the audience to use the microphones provided, stating their names and affiliation. You may wish to repeat questions so the speaker fully understands.

Finally

Thank all the speakers and thank the audience for attending.

Presenting to The Lay Public

The more specialized we become the harder it is to explain what we do, or what we mean, to members of the lay public. We develop a language specific to our area of expertise and research. Some people are good at explaining to the lay public, but it is very easy to slip into using jargon that is unfamiliar and using words that are unpronounceable. This is particularly true for the sciences, medicine and dentistry.

It is important that we can communicate with non-specialists since many committees such as interview panels, ethics committees, Internal Review Boards (IRB), and funding organizations often have lay members on them. If they cannot understand your proposal then it is less likely to succeed. It pays to avoid them having to work too hard to understand you.

Beware

Presenting to the public is common. Learn how to present without relying on jargon.

Write your talk as normal using the standard construction with a simple title, an introduction explaining what you are going to be talking about. The body section will be the most tricky since it will be the longest part and one where you are likely to lose the audience. Sum up, making it very clear what you have said and why it is important.

Use analogies

This generally works. When explaining how a molecule works, for example, you might say "*it's like a lock and key – it fits in this groove in this molecule and opens the groove up...*".

Try to gauge whether they are following you (or not) by noting their body language, facial expressions and other signs. If they are following you they will look attentive. If you have lost them, they will not be watching you so closely, and some may fall asleep! Every now and again you can say "*Does that make sense?*" or "*Please interrupt at any point if what I say is not clear*". This will work when you have audiences of up to 50 or 60 individuals but in large lecture halls this may be more tricky.

Practice with your partner or child

Perhaps once you have written your talk you could present it to one of your family members to see if they can understand what you are saying. If they get confused about some points you can try to clarify these further before you do it for real. They will soon tell you if you are using words that are not understandable to the lay public!

Impromptu Speeches

"It usually takes more than three weeks to prepare a good impromptu speech." Mark Twain (1835–1910).

"Perhaps you would like to say a few words about...?" This can be a scary experience, suddenly being put on the spot and expected to pluck a coherent speech out of thin air!

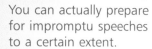
Preparation

Can you prepare for such an occasion? Actually you can. If you are at a business meeting there is a reasonable chance someone will ask you about you or your company or a product. If you know your stuff (and you should!) then it should not be too difficult to speak for a few minutes about what you do or where you see things going. It does not have to be as polished as a standard presentation. If you

suspect there is a chance you will be asked to say something, jot down some headings on index cards or piece of paper before the meeting. Then add some subheadings but not too much extra text. Just rehearse the salient points over and over a few times and that should be sufficient. When the occasion arises, you should be able to recall the large print headings and subheadings and embellish these fairly easily.

Delivery

Again, this differs from the conventional talk since you will likely launch straight into the speech. In order to crystallize your thoughts (and recall the major headings you noted down) pause for a few seconds and only start talking when you have at least the first couple of headings ready. The pause effect makes you look measured and thoughtful, and overall it makes you look in control.

If desperate

If you start to dry up and cannot think how to proceed from a certain point you could try passing the challenge to someone else by saying *"Actually, if we're discussing X, I'd like to pass this to Bob, who knows more about this than I do"*. Then pass the microphone figuratively to Bob who will need to take over.

The worst speech I can ever recall giving was at a Caravan Club meeting which was held in a field. The members were fundraising in order to buy a piece of equipment for the local hospital where I worked. They were running stalls with games and things to buy. They raised a fair bit of cash and at the end of the day they gathered round in the field and one of the senior members asked me to say a few words to the members! They had a microphone which did not work properly and it was hard to make myself heard. My speech was all over the place since my heart was racing and I was trying to hold our wriggling baby in my arms at the same time. I should have seen this coming and I could have had a speech in my head but I was ill-prepared and it showed. I have not made this mistake since!

Honesty is the best policy
If you really don't know how to talk about an item because you have forgotten the details or you just haven't a clue, you can say *"I'm sorry, I can't answer that right now but I will get back to you after the meeting once I have given it some thought."*

Summary

- Presenting one-on-one is the ideal opportunity to persuade. Deliver your pitch confidently and leave enough time for questions. Be flexible and expect interruptions

- With business presentations expect questions related to finance and profitability. You may fail if you stumble over your financial figures

- Small group discussions are perfect for teaching and information sharing. Control the group and prevent dominant members taking over. Try to get everyone involved. Some small group discussions may fail because of the personalities and local politics

- Chairing meetings requires skill. Your role as chair is as moderator, ensuring the agenda is followed and a consensus is reached. Liaise closely with the meeting secretary and send out the agenda, minutes of the previous meeting, and relevant papers well ahead of the next meeting

- An invitation to speak at an academic conference is flattering but can be a frightening experience for the novice. Good timekeeping is essential. There are always specific requirements such as presentation format, timings, dress code but this information is generally sent out to speakers before the conference. There should be no hidden surprises

- For some conferences you may need to send your presentation weeks ahead of the conference date so it pays to be organized and get your slides ready early

- International meetings are very much part of business life. These may be similar to national meetings but you must be sensitive to cultural issues which may cause offense

- Presenting to the lay public is becoming quite common, with lay members sitting on many academic and other committees. Modify your presentation so it is understood by all

- Do not be caught unawares when it comes to impromptu speeches. When done well, you will make a big impression. You *can* prepare in advance and you should always expect the unexpected!

6 Slide Design

Slides are integral to modern presentations. Slide programs make it easy to generate visuals. You should spend time developing your slides so they have a clean look with maximum impact. Avoid jazzy backgrounds, animated templates and other distracting designs.

Slide Design: General Points

"The slide that says everything says nothing."

Slides are used in virtually every business and educational presentation today. It is very difficult for most people to contemplate giving a talk without the aid of some type of visual accompaniment. There are numerous programs available for creating slides and slide shows. PowerPoint (Microsoft) has become the industry standard and there are both Windows and Mac versions available. Apple's presentation software, Keynote, is an alternative, although this only runs on a Mac.

Slide programs make is easy to create slides. They also make it easy to create really *bad* slides!

Upsides of slide software
- Complement spoken content
- Easy to use
- No longer need to make 35mm slides
- Content can be modified easily
- Can embed photos, images, video, sound, and hyperlinks
- Portable
- Can be used to print handouts
- High impact if used well

Downsides of slide software
- Can be a distraction rather than visual aid – the audience reads the words on the slides
- People get carried away and create slides that contain too much text and poor graphics
- Can be somewhat boring to look at if there are lots of slides with bullet points

Why do we cram so much onto our slides?
When we are anxious it is harder to recall information so we use our slides as the repository for all the information we *might* need during our presentation. Sometimes we feel the information is very important and we want the audience to see this rather than

just hear it. Sometimes we feel that very complex and busy slides will impress the audience more.

Keep the slides simple

- Use a plain background. White works well if you are projecting in a small room or dark if the room is large

- Lots of short slides with few words give you more flexibility

- Use only 1 or 2 fonts in a presentation

- Avoid exotic fonts – there may be fonts that you think look great but when you take the presentation to a conference the font gets substituted with Arial since the laptop at the meeting does not have your font in the font folder

- Watch colors – do not overdo it or the slides look garish

- Use images – high quality photos, vector diagrams, graphs. Try to avoid clip art – it usually looks cheap

- Avoid having bullets on every slide

- Place one blank slide (e.g. black background) at the very end of your presentation

- Avoid using "*Thank you!*" or "*Any questions?*" slides. These are fine for school but not serious presentations

Keep your slides simple, avoid exotic fonts and use good quality images.

Avoid this type of slide if at all possible!

That Presentation Sensation, Conradi & Hall, Prentice Hall, 2001

Switch Off The PC

Typing straight into PowerPoint can be tricky so try paper and pen instead.

When you are writing your talk and building your slides it is often a disadvantage to sit at the PC typing. There are too many distractions such as email, or websites that you suddenly remember to visit. Before you know it, you have wasted lots of time, grabbed some cheesy graphics and the text is long-winded and lacking direction.

There are some things you *can* do while music is playing in the background or you are sitting in front of the TV. For example, tidying up a Word document, changing formatting, looking for graphics for your talks, or creating graphs from your data. But it is much more difficult to write coherently while there are background distractions. The children's author Roald Dahl use to write in the shed at the bottom of the garden, presumably because there was no phone, TV or other things which might have prevented him writing. Try it – see if you can write better in a quiet room with a clear desk. You might be amazed at the results.

Peace

So try switching your PC off and clear your desk of clutter. Grab some paper and a pencil and start jotting down ideas for your talk. Remember the key messages, and try to bring in information, graphs, studies, images that support your argument or discussion. Use different sheets of paper for the various sections of your talk. Once you have got as many ideas down as you think are necessary for your presentation, try to order these so that they flow in a logical sequence. Before you start actually typing the slides, it might be better to use index cards. Each card represents a slide in PowerPoint. If you have a 30 minute talk, get 30 index cards in a pile and start transferring the information from your notes to the index cards.

On each card note down what graphic you think might add to the slide visually.

Check the flow

Read through your cards from beginning to end. Does it flow well? Does it get your main points across? Are your key messages clear at the end? If you are happy with the end result you can open your slide program and transfer the material.

Use a program with minimal distractions

There are programs which blot out all distractions from your screen. WriteRoom (*http://hogbaysoftware.com/products/writeroom*) makes your entire Mac screen black and text appears in green (like computers from 20 years ago). Because you cannot see any menus you tend not to worry about formatting. You are then free simply to enter text. For creative people this simple solution helps keep them on track. DarkRoom is the PC version of WriteRoom and it is worth trying the demo (*http://they.misled.us/dark-room*). Notepad for Windows is similar but you can still see your desktop and the menus.

Hot tip

If you do prefer to type your thoughts into the PC use simple uncluttered software.

This is a very simple text editor. The text is green but it can be changed to any color and any font. There are no rulers, menus or other gizmos that might otherwise impede productivity. It is designed for people who want to write novels but it can be used any time you want to blot everything out and just concentrate on the text!

PowerPoint

PowerPoint was originally designed for the Mac but was bought by Microsoft in 1987. Today there are versions of PowerPoint for both PC and Mac.

Composing your slides

Keep things simple and include only text and a few images. Video, animation, sound and live hyperlinks can be used but they create more layers of complexity.

Use your index cards or notes as content for your slides. It is best not to type your ideas straight into PowerPoint otherwise your slides end up being busy and lacking focus.

Open PowerPoint on your PC or Mac

This will take you to an untitled presentation, usually with the default Arial font and a white background. If you plan to change the fonts, background or other aspects you will need to access the **Slide Master**.

This is what you see when you first open PowerPoint. Click **Slide Master** to change the background and fonts.

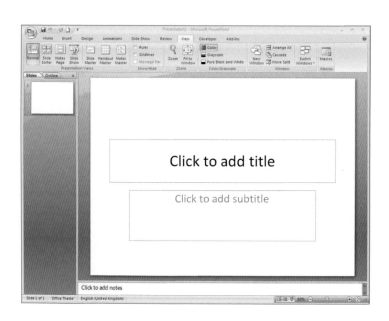

Let's change the background to blue and the font to Tahoma. You will need to change the settings for the Title slide, then apply the same settings for the other slide types you wish to use.

You can use PowerPoint's themes or choose your own background.

Here we have changed the background to blue and the font is Tahoma.

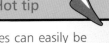
Hot tip

Themes can easily be modified if you have specific font preferences.

Now you can start entering your text into the new design. In this template each line is bulleted. You can remove bullets in the Slide Master which will result in new slides having no bullets.

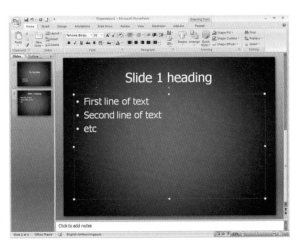

Here is the title slide, in the same style as the rest of the slides. Using the same theme throughout a presentation is important – avoid having slides with different backgrounds or fonts.

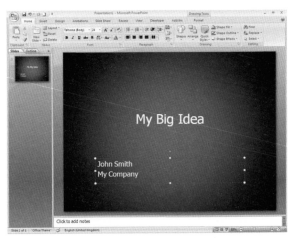

Apple Keynote

This program is similar to PowerPoint. It uses a system of Slide Masters where you will set up the design of your presentation. Once you are happy with the overall design you can start entering your text and placing graphics. Much like PowerPoint, the program comes with several predesigned templates suitable for different types of presentation. You can also purchase additional templates online from a variety of sources (the same is true of PowerPoint).

The programs are similar but not identical. PowerPoint is more commonly used in the business and academic world. If you take along a Keynote presentation to a conference the chances are you will not be able to use it since most AV departments use PCs and there is no PC version of Keynote. The best way to use Keynote, if you are determined to use it, is to take along your own Mac laptop with Keynote installed. You can plug this into the projector and show your presentation.

Workaround

Keynote allows you to export your presentation in a variety of formats. If you choose the PowerPoint option you will need to open the presentation in PowerPoint since some of the formatting may change. In addition, any fancy transitions you have used in the Keynote file will not work on the PC so try to limit your slide transitions to something simple rather than the rotating cube or complex dissolves. Finally, the Mac uses fonts in its Keynote templates that are not available on most PCs. PowerPoint will substitute a font and this may shift text and tables around. If you know you will be exporting to the PC try to stick to Arial or some other font common to both the PC and the Mac.

Hot tip

Keynote is simple to use and the presentation can be exported in a number of different formats.

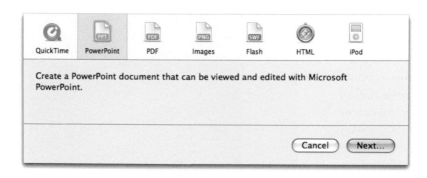

Setting up your Keynote presentation

Choose a fairly simple template. You can use Keynote's themes or choose your own background. This theme is *Letterpress* and the font is Hoefler Text.

Transitions and effects in Keynote may not transfer well to the PC.

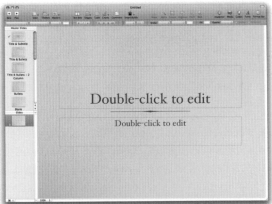

Now you can start entering your text into the new design. The template centers the lines of text, but this can be changed to force the text to the top of the box (which is more conventional).

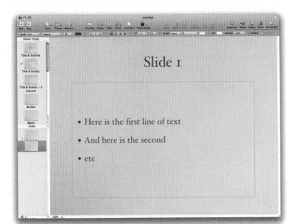

Here is the title slide, in the same style as the rest of the slides. Remember to check out the inbuilt Master Slides – there are Masters set up for text, text with images, and other designs.

Adding Images

Hot tip

Images are great for presentations but only use one per slide.

Having photos, line art or other visual material on your slides enhances the overall appearance. Too many images, however, will spoil the look, so try to use one image per slide if possible. Once your image has been added, you can position, resize and add depth by using drop shadows and other effects.

Adding images to PowerPoint

Have your image files on the desktop or a designated folder so you can find them easily.

The slide below looks pretty bare and we would like to add an image of a plant. First, locate the **Insert** button in PowerPoint. Select **Insert Picture** since we are adding a JPEG.

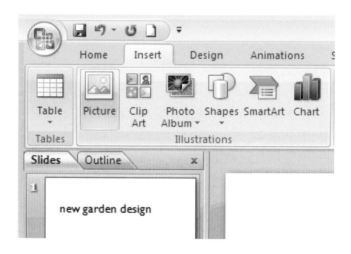

Locate the image file and insert it.

The image has been resized. Click and drag the image to any part of the slide. Choose the place which fits best.

A soft drop shadow has been added, giving the appearance of depth.

PowerPoint has lots of other effects but do not overdo these – they may detract from the simplicity of the slide.

Slide Enhancers

Beware

There are several PowerPoint add-ons but in general these do not enhance the look of your slides.

There are programs available that will work with PowerPoint, making it easier to organize your slides, and allow you to set timings for presentations, with animated backgrounds.

Serious Magic Ovation

Ovation offers preset themes such as clouds or spinning globes. Ovation imports your PowerPoint file and then gives you the option of keeping your original theme and fonts or switching to the Ovation fonts. Once the slides have been imported you can set up "Walk In" slides (for the beginning of the show) and "Exit" slides for the end of the show. Slide editing has to be done in PowerPoint so you toggle back and forth between Ovation and PowerPoint. Note, Ovation only works with Windows XP.

These show Ovation's main window and Present view (bottom).

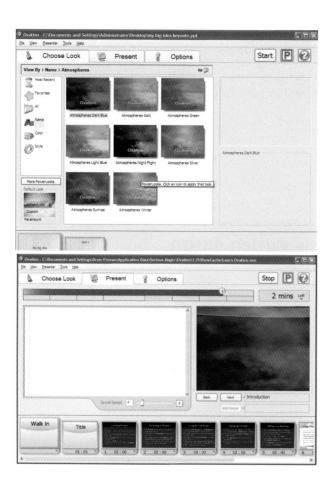

Slide Executive Desktop

This program helps you organize your PowerPoint slides. Suppose you have 3 PowerPoint files containing slides that you want to use in one new presentation. This software opens all 3 and lets you drag and drop slides from all 3 old PowerPoint files into your new file.

Here we have opened one presentation (right panel).

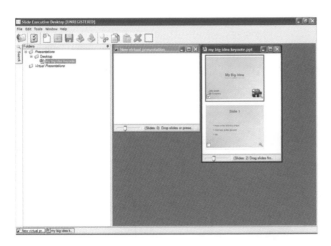

Now a second presentation has been opened and slides from both are being added to a third presentation (middle of the picture).

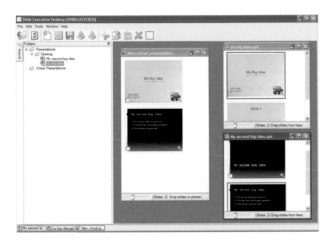

The software can be downloaded from *www.slideexecutive.com*.

Why PowerPoint Fails

Beware

The ease of PowerPoint may result in overcrowded slides. You may lose your message.

This title is a misnomer since it is not the PowerPoint that is failing – it is our ability to create good slides that fails. PowerPoint-type software is intended as an aid, and should complement what we say and reinforce messages through the use of simple text and good graphics. But many people put too much information onto the slides. The key points are much harder to see. The slide below is a great example of *too much information*!

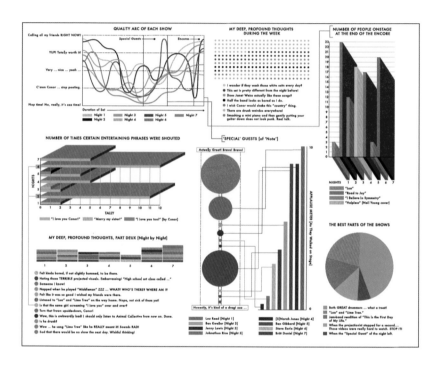

Bad slide design

The quality of slides used for presentations varies enormously. Some people use simple slides, white backgrounds and minimal text while others use animated backgrounds crammed with bullets, *sub*-bullets and even *sub–sub*-bullets! If your entire speech is on the slides there is almost little point in you being there at all.

Slide text

Keep the content simple and elaborate heavily in your spoken text. This makes your slides easy on the eye and stops the audience having to spend all their time reading (even if you say "*Don't read all the details on this slide*" they will!).

Backgrounds

Plain works best, possibly with a gradient. Darker slides with light text are great for large rooms.

Keep the bullets down

Don't spray the entire slideset with bullets. Try getting rid of them. Use another means to list items.

Below, is one of my own slides which has a distracting background and too much text. I have slimmed it down a little and toned down the background to try to improve it.

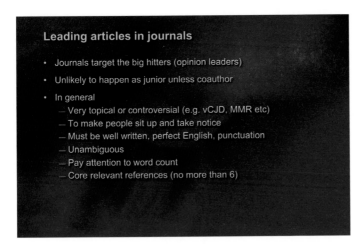

I have changed the background and removed the bullets.

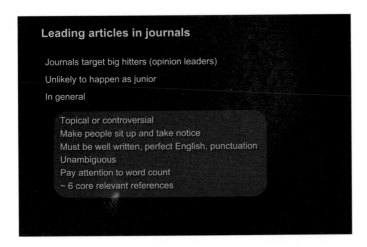

Creating High Impact Slides

Audiences like slides. It gives them something to focus on and it helps drive your message home. Highly skilled speakers hone their slides down to being so minimalistic the audience would not know what the talk was about if they had no oral presentation to accompany them. Other speakers use so much information within their slides that they, as speakers, become redundant.

You should be aiming for the middle ground, with enough information to prompt you as you go through your presentation, even if you are very nervous, and the slides should be easy on the eye.

Ideal background
Simple. Just dark or light with little else. Avoid any PowerPoint background that is animated.

Text
As little as you can get away with. Try to avoid bullets but this is easier said than done. Bullets are a fact of life and we use them in our documents, as well as our slides. Try to keep them to a minimum. Only use two fonts maximum. The text should be a reasonable size (22 points or above for body text) otherwise people at the back of the room will not be able to read the text.

Zany 3D text looks terrible. Never use this.

Spellcheck
A great presentation will be spoiled if there are typos on your slides. Either switch on the spellchecking as you type or check the entire presentation at the end.

Images
Photographs and (some) line art really helps. You can use fewer words if you use pictures. Don't mix line art, such as clip art, with photographs. Try to avoid clip art if you can.

The slide below uses a vector graphic. This type of image can be resized with no loss of sharpness (unlike a TIFF, JPEG, PNG and other formats).

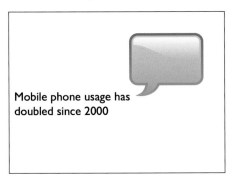

Black slide at the end

If you have your *Conclusion* slide as the very last slide, when you press advance, PowerPoint will take you out of Slide Show and into Slide Edit mode. But if you have a black blank slide at the end the screen will just turn black after you finish your presentation and this provides a much more elegant ending.

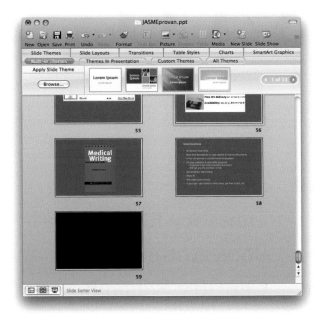

Hot tip

Include a black slide right at the end of the presentation so you can end gracefully.

Choosing Fonts

Computers are supplied with lots of fonts – too many in fact. Some are common to all platforms while others are specific to PC, Mac and other platforms. If you intend to show your slides on both PC and Mac, or design on the Mac and present with a PC or vice versa you must use a font that is common to both PC *and* Mac.

Serif versus sans serif

Serifs are the fancy embellishments common to many fonts. Times New Roman is a good example of a serif font. It works well in books, professional documents and newspapers but does not look great on the screen during a presentation.

Hot tip

Arial and other sans serifs are easy to read and are ideal for slides.

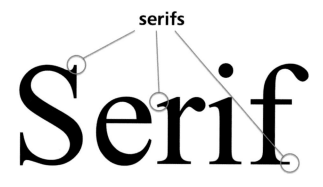

serifs

For clarity it is best to use a font which lacks serifs – sans serif. Examples include Arial, Helvetica, Tahoma, Verdana and many others.

Beware

Serif fonts are less easy to read on a screen but are great for printed documents, especially at small point sizes.

Sans Serif	Serif
Calibri	TimesNewRoman
Arial	Book Antigua
Tahoma	Century Schoolbook
Verdana	

Fonts for slides

You need to decide on your Title font as well as the Body Text font. Arial can be used for both and will provide clear text that is easy to read from the back of the room. Alternatively, you could use Tahoma or Verdana (both are Microsoft fonts).

PowerPoint and Keynote supply presentation templates that come preloaded with fonts but beware the Mac to PC substitution problem!

The ideal font for presentation slides

This is a matter of taste but general rules apply:

Beware

- Easy to read e.g. at least 36 point for Titles and 24 point for Body Text

- Contrasting color e.g. black fonts on light background and light fonts on dark background

- Keep text to a minimum

- Use the same design throughout your presentation – never switch part way through

- Avoid ComicSans – there are few fonts that are disliked as much as this one, and there is a hate campaign against it!

Avoid using a Mac-specific font or your slides will look bad when presented using a PC.

Title is 44 point Calibri

Body text is 32 point Calibri

But would work well with Arial

For extra impact why not try...

Gill Sans? A very contemporary font

Warning: avoid ComicSans at all costs!

(see http://typographica.org/000389.php)

Displaying Tables

PowerPoint and Keynote handle tables fairly well and although your message may be contained in the tables, they can look ugly.

Tables

These are used extensively in word processed documents but the same tables will look bad in a presentation. You need to aim for a simple table showing only the key information.

Start like this...

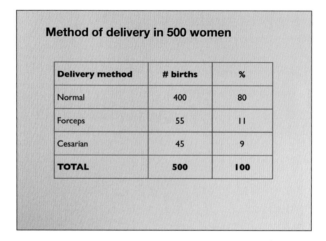

Method of delivery in 500 women

Delivery method	# births	%
Normal	400	80
Forceps	55	11
Cesarian	45	9
TOTAL	**500**	**100**

Trim down to this...

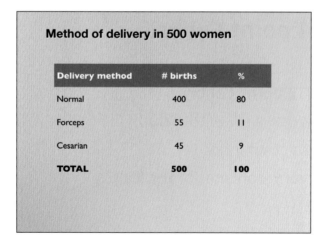

Method of delivery in 500 women

Delivery method	# births	%
Normal	400	80
Forceps	55	11
Cesarian	45	9
TOTAL	**500**	**100**

There is little clutter on the slide now and you can show exactly what you want to show.

Displaying Graphs

Instead of using a table to show your data, sometimes a graph or chart will convey the information much more dramatically. PowerPoint and Excel work hand-in-hand, and you can do some very sophisticated data manipulation. Keynote has simpler charting functions but it does produce high quality graphs.

2D or 3D

As software becomes more sophisticated we are able to view our graphs in 3D, from any angle! Whether this improves the content or impact remains to be seen. Many believe that simple 2D charts are easier to view and are more likely to convey the message you want.

Beware

Charts can be presented in 2D or 3D. In general, 2D works fine so use that.

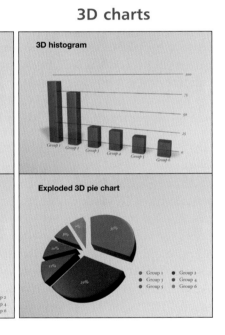

2D charts **3D charts**

Ultimately you need to decide what looks best since this is largely a question of taste. Often, something that looks stylish to one person will be seen as gratuitous and ugly to another!

If you wish to show the segments of the pie chart one at a time, or the columns on a line graph, you can use PowerPoint or Keynote's build features to show your data one step at a time. This results in a gradual building of the information and can be used as an effective way to build tension as you go through your data.

Technical Glitches

These are always waiting for the unwary! Your presentation may look great on your PC at home but when you take it to the conference it all goes horribly wrong. Why?

Corrupt files

Electromagnetic irradiation, disk errors during the copying, and other factors, can cause this. You can often see the file on the disk but when you double-click or try to open within the program you are told it is not a valid PowerPoint file. There is little you can do here except pray you have a backup with you.

CD or flash drive cannot be read

Mac users regularly take presentations to meetings where they are played on PCs. Normally there is no problem provided the CD or flash drive has been formatted to FAT32 or some format that can be read by a PC. If you inadvertently use a Mac format for the disk there is nothing you can do (unless someone in the audience has a Mac laptop and can do a quick format for you). For removable drives it is always best to use a format that can be read by all platforms and FAT32 is best.

Fonts and layout messed up

Fonts are great for expressing yourself and creating presentations which are unique to you. Unfortunately, the fonts that PowerPoint uses are those resident on the host machine. If you take your presentation to a meeting and you have used a specific typeface, unless the conference PC has that same typeface your text is going to reflow. Tables that lined up nicely at home will now look disorganized. Best rule of thumb is to stick to common fonts (Arial, and other common Windows fonts). The best way to use unusual typefaces is to project your presentation using your own laptop. Most conferences will not allow this, unfortunately.

Here is a list I made using an uncommon font					Here is a list I made using an uncommon font				
Peak count	81	135	240	188	Peak count	81	135	240	188
Change from baseline	52	118	227	173	Change from baseline 173	52	118	227	
Fold change	2.7	8.5	17	12.7	Fold change	2.7	8.5	17	12.7

Red crosses through your graphics

This again is often a Mac/PC issue. Your slides have been created on the Mac but on the PC some of the images that project beautifully on the Mac turn into white squares with red crosses through them. The other nightmare is when you see "*QuickTime and a TIFF (or JPEG) decompressor are needed to see this picture*". This occurs when images are saved in the incorrect format (CMYK instead of RGB, for example). But this error sometimes crops up for no obvious reason. If you want to be absolutely sure your presentation looks as good on the PC as it did on your Mac you should view it on a PC before you leave for the airport.

You have used the wrong version of PowerPoint

New versions of programs often save files in a different format to the old versions. PowerPoint 2007, for example, has .pptx as its proprietary format. This type of file can only be opened in PowerPoint 2007 (there is no backward compatibility). Unless the conference organizers have upgraded to the latest version of Microsoft Office (unlikely) then it is best to save as an older version of PowerPoint (2003).

Don't forget

Some visual effects don't work in older versions of PowerPoint. Save to an older version if you are unsure.

117

Soft shadows are now harsh shadows

Again, this is a compatibility problem. PowerPoint 2007 can generate some rather fancy soft shadows (and many other visual effeccts) which you can use with pictures or text. However, when you display the slides using an older version of PowerPoint your soft shadow effects will become hard lines and look very ugly. To avoid this, try not to use shadows at all then it does not matter what version of the software you use to run the show. It may be worth asking the organizers what version of the software they use.

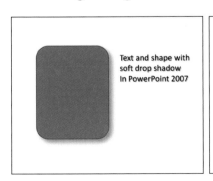

Text and shape with soft drop shadow In PowerPoint 2007

Text and shape with soft drop shadow In PowerPoint 2007

Handouts

Providing handouts is common practice for lectures, educational events at conferences and other meetings. Having a printed copy of the presentation allows the audience to listen rather than write throughout your talk. All presentation programs allow users to print their slides in a variety of formats, and in color, grayscale or black and white.

Handout purists

These people would say that your handouts should not contain your entire presentation. The set of slides you use when you give a talk should not contain *all* that you are going to say, otherwise you might as well not be there. Also there will be too much text on the slides and the audience will spend the entire time reading your slides.

Your handouts should therefore be a mini-version of your talk, containing key elements but by no means all the text and diagrams.

Handout pragmatists

We are all very busy these days and it is very difficult to find the time to generate a separate set of materials to hand out to the audience. If you only give one or two talks a year then this would be fine, but if you regularly present I suspect you would prefer not to design audience-specific handouts.

So the simplest solution is to provide the slideset as a PDF which the conference or meeting organizer can print off and place in the delegate pack for each person attending your talk. Alternatively you can give them the PowerPoint file and let them decide whether to go for full color, 3 slides on a page or 6, or whatever else they want to do with your material.

You can use the handouts too

Whenever you give a talk, have a copy of your handout in your bag when you travel. Go through your entire talk and work out the areas that cause you trouble. Maybe you cannot remember the financial details of one part of a project – write this down next to the slide. Do the same for other complex parts of your talk. Immediately before you give the talk you can then read through the difficult points again to refresh your memory. You will be able to present this with ease. You can also take the handout up to the podium with you so you can refer to it if you dry up.

Here are two examples of handouts. The 3-per-page version provides lines for people to make their own notes as you speak. The 6-per-page is more condensed and does not provide much room for writing. The color handout makes it more difficult to see some of the text, although larger text (30 points and above) will show fairly well.

 Hot tip

For teaching, provide handouts with 3 slides per page so the audience can make notes.

119

Speakers notes

There is a PowerPoint option for speakers notes (**Notes Page View**). Here you can enter the facts that you worry about forgetting. Before your presentation, instead of printing yourself handouts, print off a set of speakers notes (one slide per page) and you will have prompts for those difficult details you might forget.

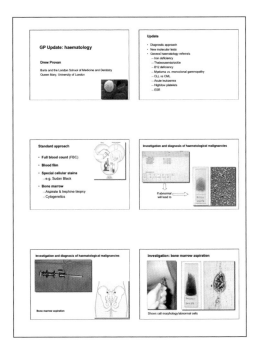

Prepare a Portable Version

Handheld devices are becoming increasing popular, initially with Palm devices, then the iPaq but more recently cell phones including the iPhone are able to display PowerPoint and Keynote files fairly effectively.

Most of these devices allow you to view the presentation but few allow editing of the content. On a small screen this is hardly surprising, and just being able to *view* the slides is a bonus. Before you step onto the podium you can review your slide content discreetly rather than shuffle through paper handouts.

PowerPoint can now be converted for a number of devices and formats including PDA, iPhone, Video, YouTube, iPod, Apple TV, MP4, AVI, WMV, BlackBerry, Zune, Pocket PC and PSP.

Conversion for PDA

If you are using a PC then the best way to get your .ppt file onto your handheld device (e.g. iPaq) is to use ActiveSync and software like Pocket Slideshow (*www.cnetx.com/slideshow/*) or Microsoft PowerPoint Mobile (*www.microsoft.com*). The software works with ActiveSync reducing the file and screen size to fit the PDA. After the file is on the PDA simply open the program and load up the file. For PDAs running other operating systems such as BlackBerry there is proprietary software that facilitates the transfer to the handheld.

Most devices that run Windows CE (a scaled-down version of Microsoft Windows) use a similar transfer method, usually involving ActiveSync.

iPod, iPod Touch and iPhone

One method of getting your files onto these devices is to use a piece of software that converts your PowerPoint file to a movie file (.mov). This can be dropped into iTunes and at the next sync

Don't forget

You can make PDA versions of your slides to review on the move.

120

of the iPod the file will be placed in the Movies folder. Load the movie and flick through your slides.

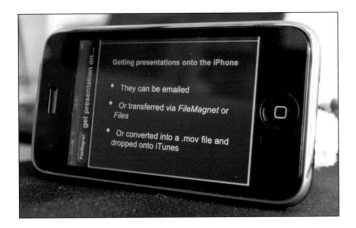

An alternative method for the iPhone is to email the .ppt file to yourself and open the file within the Mail program on the iPhone. If you need to convert your movie to fit the iPhone screen you can use the free program Handbrake (*handbrake.fr/*) which will convert for a number of devices. An alternative solution is to use FileMagnet (*www.magnetismstudios.com/FileMagnet/*) Files (*www.olivetoast.com/Files*), or Air Sharing (*www.avatron.com*).

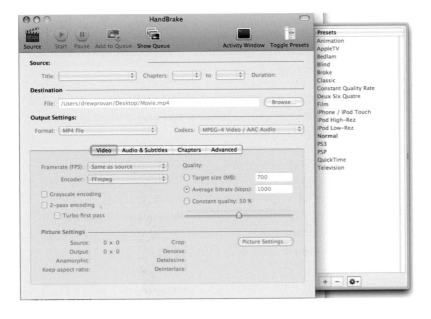

Summary

- Presenting using software such as PowerPoint or Keynote has become part of everyday life, from school children to top CEOs. These programs offer major advantages over their 35mm lantern slide counterparts – they are easy to make, easy to modify and are very portable

- Most of us make slides that are boring and over-filled with text and graphics leading to dull PowerPoint presentations

- Simple, elegant slides have more impact than those crammed with information

- Use plain backgrounds and avoid templates

- Cut down on bullet points where possible

- Use only good quality photos and other images, and avoid clip art

- Tables and charts can be used to convey large amounts of information but keep them simple

- Create your content on paper or a simple word processor first rather than type straight into PowerPoint or Keynote

- Ensure your presentation is saved in a format that can be opened on the PC where you will give your talk. If in doubt, always save backwards to an older version of the software

- Mac users should use FAT32 for flash drives, rather than the standard Mac format, to ensure the drives will mount on the PC at the meeting

- Handouts are very popular with delegates at meetings and are also very useful for you to make notes and peruse before you actually give your talk

- Handheld devices including cell phones and MP3 players are capable of storing and displaying PowerPoint and Keynote presentations. This provides another way for you to run through your presentation while you await your turn to walk up to the podium

7 Looking The Part

Try to look your best for the presentation. Nervousness is common but can be conquered.

Dress For The Occasion

It is a fact of life that audiences will judge you on appearances, so it is important to look the part and dress well. Presenting is all about performance and acting, so you should dress to impress. All eyes will be on you!

Dressing well will also give you confidence when you present, and your message will carry more weight. The audience is far more likely to be persuaded by you if you appear smartly dressed than if you turned up in a T-shirt and jeans (unless you are Steve Jobs).

In general, it is better to be slightly more dressed than your audience. For business meetings and many academic meetings, it is usual for men to wear a suit and tie. PhD students presenting scientific data in a conference could probably get away with less formal wear but even they look more impressive if they dress smartly.

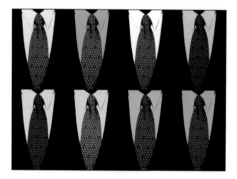

Informal meetings
If you are speaking at an internal meeting, or taking part in an advisory board or committee where the atmosphere is more casual, you could probably take off your jacket when you present and roll your sleeves up. This makes you look more relaxed which is an advantage since you are not giving an authoritative didactic lecture in this setting.

New clothes?
Some advise against wearing new clothes for presentations in case they are uncomfortable. It may be safer to wear something tried and tested that you know feels and looks good. However, wearing new clothing or shoes does give you a mental boost and if it makes you feel better about yourself, and less anxious about the

presentation, then wear a new outfit, by all means. It is generally worth keeping one or two business suits for presentations, then you can concentrate on your presentation and not about what to wear on the day

Color

Dark suits for both men and women work well. You can wear a light colored shirt, and colorful stylish tie to make an impression.

Shoes

These should be clean and not scuffed. Generally black formal-style shoes work best. Polish them if necessary. Women should avoid high heels. Flatter shoes, such as court shoes, are safer.

Don't forget

Keep your dress neutral and avoid too much jewelry.

Pockets

Normally we have items in our pockets such as handkerchiefs, money, wallets, cell phones. These are bulky and may cause bulges. To maintain the smart business look these are better left in your bag. Keep your pockets empty – this will also stop you jangling money in your pocket while you present.

Jewelry

You can wear jewelry but try to avoid large stones or very large items of jewelry, such as necklaces, since these may distract the audience.

Nerves!

Presenting is stressful – there's no two ways about it. We all feel nervous in this situation. Feeling nervous and stressed before a public speaking engagement is caused by a primitive response called "flight or fight". The whole scenario has its roots in evolution. If faced by a dangerous situation, adrenalin pours into the bloodstream from the adrenal glands, and gets the body ready to run away at high speed.

Effects of adrenalin

- Increased heart rate

- Digestion is slowed

- Blood is shunted away from less important organs, such as the stomach and other internal organs, to the muscles which need oxygen and a rich blood supply for the flight response

Outward (unwanted) signs of increased adrenalin

- Palpitations

- Dry mouth

- Tremor (fine shaking), especially of the hands and sometimes facial muscle tics

- Unsteady legs

- Sweating, nausea and sometimes vomiting

- Difficulty concentrating, or remembering lines

All of this can begin long before you are due to perform, but it certainly becomes worse immediately before you take the stage.

Tackling anxiety

Some anxiety is a good thing. It makes you perform better. Think of athletes – before a race they are anxious but are able to control the anxiety and they channel it in a positive way.

Try to appear calm – you may not feel calm, but try to look as though you are. The audience wants you to succeed and if you are outwardly relaxed, they are too.

Preparation – if you really know your speech and know your slides that will take you a long way towards gaining confidence, and you will start to relax.

Don't forget

We all get nervous – the key is to channel nervous energy into your presentation.

126

Get off to a strong start – if your first couple of slides and opening statements go well, your anxiety levels will start to drop.

Stress relievers

Try deep breathing, or stretching. Some people like taking a brisk walk to get rid of tension. The fresh air and exercise is good for you and will make your anxiety levels fall.

Alcohol

A couple of drinks will steady your nerves but what if the talk is at 9am? It might seem odd arriving smelling of alcohol. Although alcohol can help, its use is not recommended.

Drugs

Anxiety-relieving drugs such as the benzodiazepines have been used for many years to treat anxiety but they will cause sedation and drowsiness. You may feel a little more relaxed but you risk falling asleep!

Beta blockers

This type of medicine has been used by musicians, actors, presenters and other performers. It is of no value in sport since it slows the heart down. These drugs prevent adrenalin binding to its receptors, reducing the *outward* signs of anxiety. Propranolol is the drug most widely used. Beta blockers reduce the somatic manifestations of too much adrenalin – the tremor is virtually eliminated, and your heart rate will be slowed down to about 60 beats per minute. These drugs do not sedate but *they may have serious side effects* (heart failure, bronchospasm, especially if taken by people with asthma, and numerous other side effects). You should not take drugs such as these unless prescribed by your physician.

Psychological methods

Remember that what you feel is common and you are not alone in feeling anxious before a performance. Try to remain calm and outwardly confident and relaxed. The more you perform the better you become, and the lower your anxiety levels will be before giving speeches. Remember – the audience is on your side and they truly want you to succeed. They did not come to see a show that was destined to flop. Prepare well and you will have an inner confidence that your material is good and you are practiced. Good posture conveys control, and gives a more relaxed demeanor.

Beware

Avoid drinking alcohol to steady the nerves. It seldom improves performance.

Don't forget

Have you looked at your checklist to make sure you have everything needed for the talk?

As The Big Day Approaches

Recheck the date and time of the meeting. Do you know exactly where to go? If the venue is unfamiliar use Google maps or any map program to locate the venue, print off the details, and put this with your other papers for the meeting.

Handouts

Have you sent these to the meeting organizers? Maybe they will generate handouts from your PowerPoint file – was this sent off in good time? Do you have a copy of the handout to take with you along with a copy of speakers notes? If not, print these off now. Annotate the speakers notes if there are things you find difficult to remember such as financial details, study design, trial outcomes in drug trials, and so on.

USB Flash disk or CD-ROM

Have you got your talk backed up onto the media you are taking with you? If not, copy the presentation onto one (preferably two) flash disks plus a CD, just in case.

Versions

Check the version you have saved as. Although you may have bought the latest version of the software, large organizations often lag behind. If you save in the wrong format your presentation will not open on the computer at the meeting. Save in two formats at least (the latest, plus one backwards from that).

Questions

Have you thought through the likely questions that will arise? Do you have answers for these? Don't be caught out by someone asking something fairly basic and then not being able to answer it. If you were listening to this talk, what questions would *you* ask?

Ask The Organizers

Title of presentation
What is the exact title? Do you understand it? Can you live with it or do you need to modify it?

Format
Do they want a presentation, followed immediately by questions? Or will all speakers give their presentations then answer questions as a panel at the end? Is the panel expected to sit at the "top table" on the stage throughout? Or can the speakers sit in the front row with the audience?

Time
What time are you due to speak? For how long? How much of that time is for questions?

Content
What do they want you to cover in your presentation? Is there anything specific they want you to discuss, or not discuss? If the program has a specific theme they may want you to cover very specific aspects in your talk. Rather than disappoint the organizers, find out before finalizing your slides.

Type of meeting
Ask what the nature of the meeting is. What is it for? Is this a session with more than one speaker? If so, who are the others? What will they be covering in their presentations?

Audience
We have discussed this elsewhere in the book, but it is important that you know who you will be addressing. What do they know? What do they want to hear about? How many of them are there?

Handouts
Who is responsible for these? You or the organizers? Do they want 3 slides per page? Or 6?

Is there anything else they need from you?
Sometimes organizers ask for your biosketch, photograph, summary of your presentation, PDF or PowerPoint versions of the handout. Make sure they have all they need.

The Big Day!

Look after yourself

Get a good night's sleep if possible. You may be anxious but do try to rest before the event. If you have alcohol the night before take care not to overdo it. The last thing you want is a hangover on the vital day! Have breakfast before you set off even if you are not hungry. Try to eat something to settle your stomach even though the last thing you probably feel like doing is eating!

Survival kit for the day

Assemble what you need for the meeting:

- Laptop containing copy of presentation plus any other documents you might need to glance at before the talk. Don't forget the laptop charger

- Wear a wristwatch with a clear face so you can track your timing as you deliver your presentation

- USB flash drive and/or CD-ROMs

- Take the talks in multiple formats

- Laser pointer in case the one at the meeting does not work or fails part way through your talk

- Paper copy of your talk plus speakers notes, annotated with key information in case of memory lapses

- Questions that might come up, with model answers

- Hard copies of any paperwork for the meeting, location, schedule

- PDF version of your talk in case you want to review this immediately before you get up on the stage

Be early

Arrive early at the venue and look round. Meet the AV guys and learn how to use the equipment, change slides, dim the lights, use the microphone and other pieces of equipment.

Relax

Have you taken your beta blocker if you are using these? It is best to take this about one hour ahead of your talk.

Run through the talk one last time.

8 Delivery

Delivering the speech is one component of your performance. You also need to master the art of using the microphone, laser pointer and other equipment. You should also learn techniques that will help you deliver your talk without having to resort to notes or reading from a script. Finally, you should work out strategies to help you end your presentation well.

Initial Checklist

You should double-check the running order of the program. When are you due to speak? Are you the first or last speaker? Introduce yourself to the chairman or the person who will be introducing you. Have they got the right information about you, who you are, what company or organization you represent and what you will be discussing in your presentation? Correct any inaccuracies and provide additional information as required.

Slide changers

There are various gadgets on the market that plug into the laptop allowing you to change your PowerPoint slides wirelessly. This avoids you having to stand near the laptop pressing a key each time you want to move to the next slide. These devices are cheap and use a USB receiver that plugs into the USB slot on the laptop. Often the remotes function both as slide changer and laser pointer – but you need to remember not to press the slide change button every time you want to use the laser pointer.

Don't forget

Grab a bottle or glass of water and keep it close in case your mouth dries up.

Water

Pour a glass of water before the proceedings start, then when it's your turn to get up to the podium you can take it with you. Many of us suffer with a dry mouth especially at the beginning of a presentation, when the adrenalin dries our mouth up. Having a sip of water right at the start of the talk helps this.

Last minute check

You may feel the urge to visit the rest room – this is mainly caused by nerves. While you are there, check your tie (straight?), pockets, hair and satisfy yourself that you look smart and ready to go. Take some deep breaths while you are there.

Don't Dim Those Lights!

It happens time and time again. Just before you give your talk, the main lights are dimmed right down. You are in position behind the podium and begin your presentation. The problem is that the audience have no option but to stare ahead at the slides since they cannot see you. You could almost be in another room and give the talk and they would not notice any difference!

Hot tip

Try to keep the lights up so you can be seen. This helps you interact with the audience.

133

At major conferences, logistics like lighting are pretty much out of our control. They decide what they want and we need to go along with it.

For smaller meetings, however, you can ask that the lights not be dimmed so the audience can watch you and glance at the slides as you go through your talk. This allows you to maintain good eye contact with the audience. You can use your hands for emphasis giving a much more engaging presentation. You could opt to move away from the podium altogether and really engage them. But you can only really do this if the lights are not dimmed like a darkroom!

When the lights should be dimmed

Some presentations involving photographic material, such as photomicrographs of cells, or x-rays, CT or MRI scans are more effective when the room is dark. In very light sunny rooms the audience will not be able to see the details on the images.

Create a Strong Start

How you actually begin depends on the type of meeting you are attending. Presenting is an act and you are an actor. You are performing for the audience but you do need to remain very much *you*. Often the audience we are addressing knows us, so it would look a bit odd if we suddenly started speaking like a Shakespearean actor in *Hamlet*! Try to speak as you normally would in conversation. Imagine you are having a chat with the audience but speak a little more slowly and deliberately than you normally would.

I am happy to be here

At that precise moment you may not be happy, but try to ooze warmth and appreciation for the opportunity to come and talk to them about this since it is very important to you, and you want to share it with them.

Formal meeting

If you are speaking at a major conference, the conventional start is something like

"Mr Chairman, ladies and gentlemen: I would like to thank the organizers for the kind offer to speak at this meeting. It is a pleasure to be here and to share some of our latest data on ..."

"I am delighted to be able to share..."

"Thank you for the kind invitation to speak at this meeting. During this presentation I would like to show you some of ..."

"In this 30 minute presentation I would like to cover ..."

Then you need to get to your first slide which will generally be an outline of the content of your presentation:

"I thought the best way of approaching this would be to briefly talk about X, before moving on to share some of our key data relating to Y ..."

"In this short presentation, I will tell you about X, Y and Z. So let's start with X. This first slide shows..."

By now you will have got over your initial nerves, heard your own voice, gauged the audience and got them hooked. Your presentation should now flow smoothly.

Talk to The Audience

It's not one-on-one but try to speak as though it is. Try to avoid the "them" and "us" where you are behind a firewall bombarding them with information. They want to engage with you and to be involved in your presentation.

It is easier said than done, but try to be as conversational as you can manage. Imagine you are talking to a colleague rather than a room full of listeners.

Scan the room – make them feel like you are talking to each and every one of them. Avoid talking only to a couple of people in the front row. It is impossible to look at each person in the audience but if you divide them into sections – right, center and left, you can direct your attention throughout the talk to each section. This makes them feel that you have not forgotten them and they will be much more likely to pay attention.

135

For difficult parts of your presentation, try to keep it chatty:

"This is a tricky diagram to understand so let's take a few minutes going through the various items on this slide."

From time to time you can say *"Does that make sense?"* then move on to the next point. If you delay too long someone may put their hand up and say *"No, it doesn't"*!

Jokes and Humor

Jokes

You have not been hired as a comedian so you don't need to feel you have to be one! Jokes are difficult to manage during a presentation. They are deeply rooted in culture and there's a strong chance that your joke will not work for your audience.

Never tell a joke at the beginning of a speech – if it fails you will never recover. Jokes are not suitable for most presentations so avoid at all costs!

Beware

Telling jokes is high-risk but humor is acceptable.

Is it safe to use humor?

Humor, on the other hand, is fine. For example you could share an observation that is humorous for example, "*Goodness knows how they got away with this one but they did X experiment and amazingly it worked and this lead to Y!*" It's amusing but it is not a joke.

Self-deprecating humor is fine as long as it is not overdone. The audience generally likes this since it shows you to have human failings and they will empathize with you.

Humorous stories often work, and audiences like listening to stories:

"*I must tell you about one particular patient I saw who ...*".

Funny quotes

Funny quotations are useful if you can find these

- *www.amusingquotes.com*

- *www.short-funny-quotes.com*

Overall, if you are a very confident speaker you could try mixing some humor into your presentations. Your confidence will not be dented if these fall flat. If you are a less experienced speaker it is safer to stay away from humor altogether.

Less is More

This is an old adage but is very true. Instinctively we try to pack our presentations with:

- Lots of slides

- Lots of text and graphics on our slides

- Lots of words to accompany the many slides

The problem is that the audience will be reading like crazy while you are talking non-stop! They will not be listening to you at all, and any emphasis you put on specific items will be missed.

Stand back

While you are putting your slides together, decide how many you actually can use during your talk. If your presentation is 20 minutes you should probably really have no more than 20 slides, unless you have very few words per slide. One is your Title slide, one is for the Conclusion and there's one black slide at the end. So overall you will have about 18 slides to play with.

How much text have you put on the slides? Can you remove some? At least get rid of the sub-bullets. Try to simplify your slides but leave sufficient text on the slide to act as a prompt for you. The slide below needs *major* pruning!

Scenario Visualization – Why & When?

- To develop a scenario visualization technique to support communication between different stakeholders when evaluating scenarios
  - Ambiguity of the text-based scenarios
  - Communication problems between different stakeholders (users, developers, usability experts)
    - Particularly to support users involvement
    - Also among designers to evaluate design ideas, to check for coherence and completeness
  - Cost-effective, flexible, fast, easy to use tool supporting iterative development, rapid iteration (easy to create and modify) during early phases
  - Easy to distribute among stakeholders

How many graphics are on each slide? If more than one, try to reduce to a single image.

Laser Pointers

Long ago when we used 35mm slides in projectors we used wooden sticks to point to things on the screen. Once we had the light amplification by stimulated emission from radiation (i.e. *laser*!) we were able to stand well away from the screen and still point things out to our audiences.

When they were first available they were large heavy cylindrical devices that had to be plugged into the mains but like cell phones they have become very small and run on standard batteries. Most of these emit red light but green ones do exist. The idea behind them is that when you want to point to something on your slide you press the button and project a red dot onto the slide so the audience knows where to focus their eyes.

But presenters misuse the laser pointer and irritate the audience.

So, in general

DO

- Keep the pointer off until just below the level of the slide then put it on. You are supposed to draw to beam up the slide from the bottom to the place you want to highlight then press off

- Use the laser pointer relatively sparingly

- Make sure your hand is steady – these pointers emphasize any tremor you may have. If necessary, rest the hand holding the laser on the other arm. This diminishes any shake

- Take care you do not move away from the podium microphone or you will not be heard

DO NOT

- Point to every word

- Go along all lines of text on the slides

- Jump all over the slide or draw large endless circles round the words

- Point abstractedly at the slide

- Point the beam at the audience – these lasers can cause retinal damage

Microphones

These are very useful in large rooms since it avoids you having to shout the whole way through your presentation. The problem is very few of us have been trained to use one so it is not surprising that microphone problems are common at conventions, conferences and other large meetings.

How close to stand from the mike
If you are very close, the audience will hear lots of bangs and pops and you will end up sounding like a hip-hop artist. If you are too far away the mike will not pick up your voice.

Podium microphone
These are mounted on stands fixed to the podium. Their range of movement is limited. If you face the mike it will pick up your voice but if you turn your head the sound level will drop.

If you are using the podium mike, stay a few inches away from it, and face the microphone at all times. Avoid talking too much when your head is turned.

Lapel mike
These are small mikes that are clipped onto your lapel or tie. These can be wired but most of the newer ones are wireless. These allow you to move around freely and the sound level stays constant. Remember to switch it off if you visit the rest room.

Hand held
You can hold one of these while you talk. They are useful for Jerry Springer-type motivational talks! In general, these are for the audience where AV staff will wander round lecture halls at conferences and if an audience member wishes to speak they are handed a hand held mike.

Hot tip

When using a fixed microphone try to keep looking forward or the volume will vary.

Bad Habits

We all have bad habits. Some are minor and do not cause problems during presentations. Others are more grating and irritate the audience. The best way to tell what your own bad habits are is to ask a colleague (who may not tell you the truth) or video yourself giving a presentation.

Habits to avoid

- Playing with hair

- Avoiding eye contact, keeping your back to the audience

- *Um, er* – this is very annoying especially if you do this throughout your talk. Learn to stop doing this

- Reading a script – don't do this. Understandably you are anxious and may feel that having a script may help you get your message across better. However, to the audience it makes your talk boring and robotic. You will not be convincing if you simply read a script unless you are a trained newsreader who is used to following an autocue

- The monotone drone

- Hands flailing – try to control your hands and use them effectively to punctuate your presentation and help drive your message home. Don't just wave them around

- Forgetting to pause – having some pauses is very helpful - it helps get your message across

- Pacing the stage – off-putting, try to avoid

- Playing with jewelry

- Constantly adjusting your spectacles

- Jingling coins in your pockets

Keep to Time

Time management is critical if you are to become an effective speaker. Trying to show 60 slides in a 30 minute presentation will never work, you will overrun and alienate the audience. Aim to finish on time or even earlier – the audience will never object to any speaker who finishes before the allotted time.

Practice and rehearsal are important if you are to ensure your timing is slick. When we practice alone we tend to rush through the presentation and use up less time than the actual event. Some of your slides may have complicated diagrams or graphics and you will need to explain these to the audience. Work out how long it will take to explain a diagram. Use a stop watch if that helps.

Hot tip

Keep to time by rehearsing so you can gauge how long your presentation will take.

30 minute presentation:

1   Introduction ~ 5 minutes

2   Main body of talk ~ 20 minutes

3   Conclusion ~ 5 minutes

Time yourself during the actual presentation
When you reach the podium remove your wrist watch and place it on the podium.

Write down the time you must stop. Sometimes meetings fail to run perfectly to time so if you start late, note down the new time you should finish. For example, if you are talking for 30 minutes and were due to start at 2pm but started at 2.10pm write down "2.40" and put a ring around it so it stands out.

Half way
Learn to work out the half way point in your talks. Which slide is the half point slide? Learn which one this is so that when it appears during your presentation you know "*I am half way through my time now*". This is quite difficult, especially if you are nervous, and you may not recognize you are half way, but with practice you will become more adept at recognizing the mid-point.

Don't Read The Slides

Rule number one

Do not read the slides! If you do, you will come over as being false, boring and monotonous. Of course, if you are reading the autocue and are a trained presenter, this is allowed! Listening to anxious presenters read the slides out loud is very tedious.

With practice and rehearsal you will not need a script. Knowing your material well, and rehearsing your speech several times should give you the confidence to get up and talk without any need for a script.

Master your subject

If you are presenting on something you know well you are much less likely to read the slide content. The title of each slide should be sufficient to generate enough spontaneous speech. As the presenter, you should know more than the audience, after all, you have been invited to present to an audience and if they knew all about the subject there would be little need for a presentation.

Believe in yourself

Self-belief is very important here. You have the knowledge, you wrote the presentation and the PowerPoint slides so there is no reason why you should dry up or need to resort to reading the slides line by line.

PowerPoint is a visual aid. It is not an autocue. The words on the slides are there to enforce what you say and reinforce your message. The slides are not really there to show everything you are going to say during your presentation.

Rehearsal

This has been stated several times in the book, and I make no apology for repeating it again: practicing your presentation many times helps you construct good sentences, helps you to be confident and reinforces the content of your presentation. As each slide appears you should instinctively know what to say. The audience can read through the handouts later so what you say need not match the slide content completely.

Conclusion slide

Many presenters seem to feel it is fine to read the *Conclusion* slide verbatim. I am not sure why this is but I would recommend paraphrasing what the *Conclusion* says. But do not read the slide.

Don't forget

Practicing helps you dispense with the need for notes or a script.

Beware

Never read a script to the audience – this makes for a very boring talk which lacks spontaneity.

Memory Aids

You may feel you want to take notes to the podium with you, to jog your memory if you lapse during the presentation. What kind of notes would you use? Handwritten? The PowerPoint or Keynote speakers notes? If you use the latter, you will need to turn the page every time you change slides. But what generally happens is that you get on a roll, proceed well through the talk and forget to turn the page. When you get stuck you glance down and find the printed page does not match the slide. So you panic!

Speakers notes are excellent for reading through before you give your talk. It embeds the words in your memory and makes your talk appear smoother. They are not good notes for the podium. Instead, it is better to jot down things that you *must* remember onto a piece of card or small piece of paper. Place this on the podium when you get to it, next to your watch and glance at it from time to time. Then when you get to the end of your talk you can say "*Oh, and before I forget, our website address is www....*".

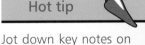

Hot tip

Jot down key notes on index cards and glance down at them every now and again.

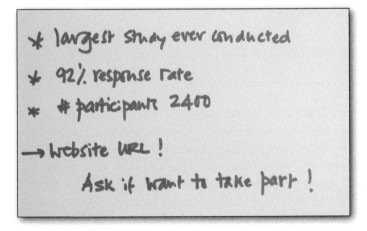

* largest study ever conducted
* 92% response rate
* # participants 2400
→ website URL !
    Ask if want to take part !

Index cards

We used these to plan the presentation, but they are also very useful as memory aids during your presentation. Use one index card per slide. Write down (in large letters) a couple of key points about each slide. If you staple them together, you can turn over the top card every time you change slide. A quick glance down at the card will help you tell the audience about specific facts. If you prefer to have the cards loose, number them so you can keep them in the same order as your slides. If your PowerPoint slides are numbered you can keep both slides and cards synchronized.

Voice Control

When you watch TV presenters notice how they vary the pitch and speed at which they present. Notice too how they introduce pauses. Good presenters use this technique for maximum impact.

Pauses

When you reach a point which you want to get across strongly to the audience you might say something like

"... and this is the ONLY model that can be recycled safely..." – then PAUSE for 5 seconds – look round the room – then move to the next slide.

Some presenters use even longer pauses but this is very difficult to do. We feel foolish not talking and we worry that the audience might think we have forgotten what we want to say, but long pauses create tension and drama.

You might also try the pause with a blank slide for even more impact!

Robots

Try to keep your voice conversational not monotonous or robotic. Stress certain parts of your sentences, for example

"... and this is the ONLY model that can ..."

Practice in front of a mirror

You may feel foolish doing this, but it works. Choose a time when the house or office is empty and no-one will walk in on you! Talk to your reflection. Give your whole presentation to your reflection and try to impress upon the image in the mirror how important the points are, be passionate and use hand gestures. Assess your overall image. Do you look convincing? Fired up? Do the gestures work well or are they too much? Change the pitch of your voice and imagine you are the best salesperson ever. Are *you* persuaded?

Video yourself

Present your talk to video. Get your camcorder out and position it so you can be seen from the waist up. Deliver your talk using the intonation, stresses and changes in pitch that you would naturally use when you present for real. Play it back and see how animated (or unanimated!) you are. Consciously try to improve your technique and re-record yourself. Getting better? If need be you could seek advice from a voice coach but this is seldom necessary.

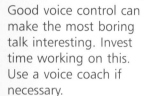

Hot tip

Good voice control can make the most boring talk interesting. Invest time working on this. Use a voice coach if necessary.

All Good Things Come to an End

You had a strong start, and the main body of the talk went really well. But how do you finish so that you leave a strong impression with key messages that have really hit home? People often listen to the first couple of minutes then the last part of a presentation.

It is doubly important that you leave a strong impression at the end because quite commonly as soon as the audience sees the word "Conclusion" they wake up (if they were asleep – which is not uncommon), start shuffling papers, put their notepads and pens in their bags and get ready to leave. In major conferences some of the audience may get up out of their seats and start heading for the door!

Key messages
The concluding slide will contain the *essence* of your presentation. It will also contain the key messages that you want the audience to remember long after the presentation is over.

Conclusion slide
- Keep it brief

- No more than 6 lines of text, avoiding long sentences

- Add no new material at this stage. Just reiterate points already made in the presentation

- Place particular emphasis on the key messages

What to say when the Conclusion slide is shown
"So what we have seen is ..."

"What I have shown you in this presentation is A, B and C ..."

"I have provided you with an overview of where we are with this product. It can do X, Y and Z and will change the way we ..."

Finally
"Thank you for your attention. I would be very happy to take questions from the audience".

Never
Just end and wait – the audience will not know what to do or when to clap.

"Well, that's about it. I have no more slides"

Summary

- Re-check all details so you know exactly what you are doing and when you are doing it

- Introduce yourself to the chairman to ensure he or she knows who you are and can introduce you appropriately

- Before you speak, make sure you are comfortable – check your appearance in a mirror before you take the stage

- Have a glass of water to hand when you talk in case your mouth dries up

- Try to keep the lights up when you talk or the audience will only see your slides

- Creating a strong start puts you in the driving seat and boosts your confidence

- Practice your opening statement and get it as near perfect as possible. The rest should then follow

- Engage the audience and talk to them to keep their attention

- Jokes are not advisable for a presentation but humor generally goes down well

- Laser pointers are useful to highlight key points on slides but are best used sparingly

- Using a microphone is harder than it looks. Ask the AV staff how to use the one provided for you

- Work out what bad habits you have when you present, and try to tackle these

- Calculate the time you need for your presentation and ensure you stick to it – if you finish early no-one will complain

- Avoid reading a script to the audience – it creates a bad impression and the audience will find you less convincing

- Notes can be useful for jogging your memory but keep them short, if possible to a single sheet

- Voice control techniques are essential if you want your speech to be engaging

9 Using Different Media

Besides standing up in front of an audience and speaking, there are many other ways to deliver a pitch. This includes presenting by phone, video or over the Internet.

Insert Video Into Slideshow

Some presentations demand the use of video as well as static images and text. There are various ways video images can be shown to your audience. One option might be to project slides from PowerPoint or Keynote on one screen and display video footage on the other.

If the piece of video is relatively short, it would be better to simply insert the video footage into PowerPoint or Keynote and play the movie within your slide.

What types of video can PowerPoint display?

Windows PowerPoint can play a number of formats (AIFF, AU, MP3, WAV, WMA, ASF, AVI, MPG, MPEG, WMV, and Flash). The Mac version can project Quicktime (.mov), WMV, WAV (sound only), WMA (sound only).

Getting video into PowerPoint

Unlike static images such as photos, video is not embedded within the PowerPoint file but linked to it. This is important, because if you rush off to show your slides but have not copied the video file to the same folder as the PowerPoint file, you will be disappointed when it comes time to show the film – it will not be there!

 Generate a slide which will show the video. Ensure the video file is in the same folder as the PowerPoint file and choose **Insert – video – from file** and select the file

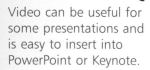
Hot tip
Video can be useful for some presentations and is easy to insert into PowerPoint or Keynote.

Beware
Keep the video file in the same folder as the PowerPoint file or it will not play.

new garden design

2 You will be asked whether you want to play the video automatically or when you click the mouse. Choose the method which you wish to use

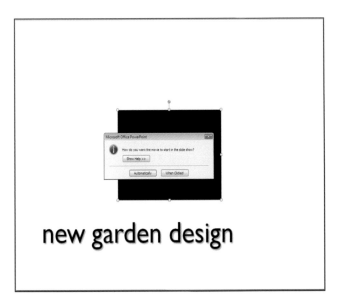

3 Play the slideshow to check the video plays as expected

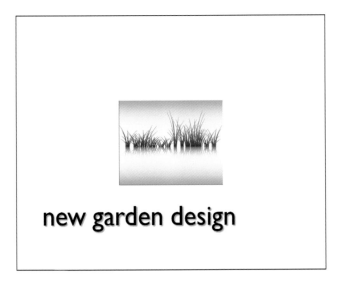

Split Projection

As the name suggests split projection involves the use of two projectors and two screens (some projectors can show two different images at the same time). This form of projection is not commonly used, but can be useful if the speaker wants to present slides containing information on one screen and an image or video on the other. In a standard presentation images and text are mixed on the same slide, but if you need to make the image fill the *entire* screen it will leave no room for words.

Presentations where split projection may be useful

- Biology or science where you need to show video of a process while you talk

- Medicine where you want to discuss a procedure such as a surgical operation. This form of projection would only be useful if the procedure is long and there is a major need to display text slides at the same time. The same effect could be obtained by simply showing the video and talking.

Only use this form of projection if you know exactly what you are doing and have mastered the art of coordinating two laptops and two projectors at the same time! The last thing you want is for the two to go out of sync!

You will need to let the conference or meeting organizers know well in advance if you wish to use split projection since it will need to be set up for you.

I suspect this is used by some presenters to show off and my advice would be to avoid this method of presenting!

Using Hyperlinks

We are familiar with hyperlinks on web pages. Clicking on a link will take us to another part of the site or a new site. The same can be achieved in PowerPoint or Keynote: clicking on a visible or invisible button (hyperlink) will take you to another slide.

Why would you want to do this? You may be teaching in a school or college and wish to quiz the audience. You can set the questions up on the main slide and include hyperlinks to the corresponding answer slides.

Using hyperlinks

Set up your slide with questions, and design separate slides for the correct and incorrect answers.

Go to **Tools** and set up the **Custom** action buttons as shown, then specify the action to be taken when the button is clicked during the presentation (in our case we want to show a specific slide in the set).

The slide below shows the question with 3 possible answers. One is correct and this hyperlinks to a slide

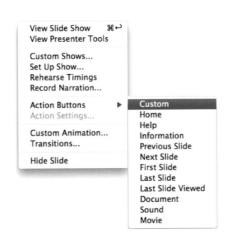

Hot tip

Hyperlinks are useful for teaching slides and save you having to manually find the right slides.

151

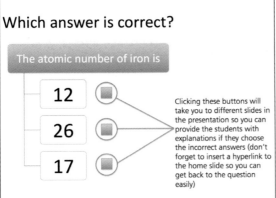

Which answer is correct?

The atomic number of iron is

12

26

17

Clicking these buttons will take you to different slides in the presentation so you can provide the students with explanations if they choose the incorrect answers (don't forget to insert a hyperlink to the home slide so you can get back to the question easily)

reinforcing the correct answer. Two are incorrect and the true atomic weights are given in the explanatory slides. Include buttons to take you back to the question slide.

Phone Presentations

Presenting in a telephone conference is another form of virtual presentation. These are popular in the business world but less so in academia and education. It allows several people in various locations or countries to "get together" without actually being in the same room. Providing the conference is planned carefully, and people adjust their presenting style to suit this format, these meetings can be very useful.

Telephone conferencing cuts down travel costs and is fairly useful if the rules are followed. It cannot be a free-for-all or there will be anarchy and no-one will have control!

In addition to voice audio, telephone conferences can also be used to present data, for example, in PowerPoint or other programs. Lotus SameTime is popular with some companies but there are many providers of programs that allow the simultaneous display of visual material.

Are you the leader?

Normally one person has to organize the telecon and is the leader. This person will have a leader "PIN" – basically a number which he or she has to enter after dialling the conference hosting company telephone number. Others will dial in at the same time and enter the predefined "Conference Code" which allows access to the telecon.

Basics of running a telecon

- The leader should introduce himself or herself and thank everyone for joining the conference

- The others should state their names and who they represent

- An agenda needs to be prepared in advance and sent to the participants ahead of the meeting, with timings shown

- Supporting documents should be sent ahead of the meeting, allowing the participants time to read the content

- If you have PowerPoint slides you wish to go through, send these before the meeting. When the telephone conference starts ask people to open the PowerPoint document

- When taking people through a PowerPoint presentation use numbered slides so you can say "*I am now moving to the next slide which should be Slide 7*", or whatever slide you are viewing on your PC. (Or you can project over the Internet)

- If you are presenting, make yourself slow down and leave pauses after each sentence if possible

- This also allows time for people to ask questions before you move to the next slide

- All participants may speak but only one at a time – it is very difficult to follow what is being said if two people try to talk

- Speech needs to be very clear and slower than usual since the participants cannot see each other

- Background noise is distracting so switch the phone to mute when you are not speaking (#6 is often the code to mute your receiver). It is not uncommon to hear sirens, lawn mowers and people's children talking in the background!

- Invest in a headset for your phone. Many of these have background noise canceling options

- At the end of the telecon the leader should wrap up the meeting, ask if there are any final points and thank everyone for attending

- The leader should make a list of off-line actions, such as emailing other documents to the group, calling people back at a later time so they can chat one-on-one about specific items

- The leader should also arrange the next telecon with the group if there is to be a follow-up conference

Don't forget

Send all papers, presentations and relevant documents ahead of the meeting.

Flip Charts

These are essentially large notepads on stands. They are cheap and rely on no complex technology.

Where a flip chart is useful

- Meetings with 6–30 people
- Informal meetings
- Small business meetings
- Teaching
- Brainstorming
- Sales meetings
- Any meeting with a high level of audience participation

Hot tip

Don't underestimate the usefulness of flip charts. They are cheap and flexible.

Beware

Make sure you can write neatly.

Requirements

- Thick felt-tip marker pens
- You must be able to write in large letters and clearly
- Avoid too many words on the page
- No more than 2 colors
- Only use the top two thirds of the page

Advantages

- Can explain details gradually since the audience is not shown everything at once

- You can write notes for yourself in pencil at the top of each sheet – this can be seen by you but not the audience

- Audience can work things out in real time and can be asked to contribute to what is written

- Can "park" items on separate sheet and come back to those later

- Can save all the pages and use for write-up later

- Can stick all pages to the wall, and a walk-through of all that was discussed can be presented back to the participants

- Useful for breakout discussions – each group can be given its own flip chart. Later, the spokesperson for each group can use the flip chart to present back to the whole group

Disadvantages

- Often seen as cheap

- If text too small cannot be seen by whole group

- No use for large audiences

- Cannot display photos or graphics easily (unless pre-printed)

- Often the text is difficult to read unless the presenter has good handwriting

Checklist

- Ensure the pad has enough fresh unused pages

- Do the pens work and have you got enough?

- Make sure stand is steady and placed where the audience can see the chart

- Don't talk while you write – your back will be to the audience and they will not be able to hear you clearly

- Don't get in the way of the flip chart or you will obscure the content on the page

Whiteboards & Blackboards

These have been around for a long time and were very popular in schools until fairly recently when electronic whiteboards took over. They are not used much in the business world but remain in use by academics in universities and colleges.

These provide a cheaper alternative to flip charts and are used in much the same way. There is a gradual showing of information by the presenter with heavy reliance on audience participation.

What do you need?

● Your presentation must be planned

● Have speakers notes nearby so you can follow the agenda you set yourself and ensure you do not miss out any key messages

● Supply of chalk or dry-wipe marker pens that work

● Reasonable handwriting and the ability to write in large letters that can be seen by the whole audience

Disadvantages

● Cannot take the pages away for writing up later – you need to make notes as you go along

● Sometimes difficult to read what is written

● Limited space and you need to erase previous content

Overhead Projectors

The "OHP" is old technology, but remains much loved by many academics. These are not popular in business but are used in schools, colleges and universities. They pre-dated PowerPoint and allowed teachers to present pre-written material to a large audience, for example, in a lecture theater. The information was generally painstakingly handwritten by the lecturer in felt tip pens especially designed to write on the plastic ("acetate") sheets.

Don't forget

In the time it takes to make the OHP slides you could have used PowerPoint.

Advantages

Suits any size group

Cheap

Requires little technical expertise

Can be shown line by line if you cover up text with paper

Can be written in real-time, like a flip chart

Disadvantages

Lose impact if text not clear

Looks cheap

Sheets often placed on OHP crooked

Sheets get lost or mixed up – which ones still to show?

Cannot display complex graphics or video

Using the OHP

- Place near the projection screen aiming to fill the screen
- Focus the lens and clean the horizontal stage
- Place the acetates on the OHP stage squarely
- Stand to one side when you present – do not block the screen
- Point words out using a pen or pencil and touch the acetate (not the screen)

Video Conferencing

This is a high tech and expensive method of presenting to an audience who may be scattered all over the world. Video conferencing allows real-time chat with video. Text and other visual material such as electronic whiteboards and PowerPoint can also be used at the same time. Their use is increasing as the price of technology drops and Internet speeds get higher. A video conference is more useful than a telephone conference because it allows face-to-face interaction between the participants. Non-verbal cues are now available to the audience and this makes video conferencing incredibly useful.

This technology can be used to present information to one person or to hundreds of people at the same time. Video conferencing has become popular in most professions, including politics, education, business, medicine and science.

Running a video conference can be very productive but unlike a standard meeting, video conferencing needs much preparation to ensure everything works and all the participants know what is expected of them.

Video conference hosting companies are abundant but they are expensive since they take care of all the logistics for you. To set up your own video conference you could try Skype, iChat or other cheaper software solutions.

Basics

If two people in different locations are taking part in a video conference each person will need a room with an LCD projector hooked up to a laptop which has Internet access (or at least access to a network for transmitting the signal) and a webcam or digital video camera. This would be a fairly basic set-up. Many companies now have video conferencing suites set up. These have state-of-the-art digital video, expensive projectors and screens. The rooms are generally designed so that the acoustics are optimal, with no echo. The lighting is also optimized so that participants can be seen clearly without lighting artefacts.

Hot tip

The video conference room should be plain with no distracting mirrored surfaces.

Requirements

- A facilitator is useful if you have one – these people are trained to use the facilities and help participants get the most out of video conferences

- Clear agenda sent out in advance with timings shown

- Make sure the time zone is clearly indicated especially if involving countries in different time zones

- Webcam and rooms for participants

- LCD projector, screen or monitor, laptop

- Name tents (folded cards with participants' names clearly shown in large font)

- Uncluttered room – remove mirrors, glaring surfaces

- Encourage the participants to wear neutral (non-striped) clothes to avoid producing distracting effects on the screen

Running the conference

- Practice beforehand to make sure all the equipment works and you know how to use it

- Participants should face the camera when talking

- If you are using PowerPoint, make sure the slides are numbered

- Use large fonts and make sure the slides are clear

Webcasts

Hot tip

Run through your talk several times so it is fairly word perfect before you start the webcast.

As the name suggests these are Internet-based broadcasts that can be given in real-time, or can be recorded in advance. They are fairly cheap to make and are popular in business, education, the media and music industry (*Live8*, for example hosted real-time webcasts of the concerts).

The technology involves creating an audiovisual presentation which is streamed to the viewer's computer. It does not have to be downloaded and watched later. In fact, streaming the content means that nothing has to be downloaded to the audience's computer.

There are webcasting companies who can help you put your webcast together. They use software specifically designed for webcasting to pre-invited audiences. In the business world you might have 20 invitees from around the world. How do you know they have logged in to your live webcast? The webcasting company software usually includes a panel on one side of the screen that shows the names of the participants as they join the live webcast. You then know exactly who is present and who has not logged in to hear you speak.

Webcasts can be viewed by participants using their own PC or several people can get together in one room.

As a presenter
This can be quite a stressful experience, since a live webcast has to begin at the allotted time, and you know that once you start you cannot stop! So get everything ready before you start.

- Make sure you have some water near you in case your mouth dries up

- You will most likely be at your desk in front of a PC with the webcast software running. You will see your slides in a panel, and there will be other panels containing the participants' names, and other information

- Whether live or recorded, you will need a set of slides if you are giving a PowerPoint style presentation

- Make sure the content is crystal clear and you have not cluttered the slides, much as you would for any other slide presentation

- Make yourself notes and have these in front of you

- Use index cards numbered the same as the slides. You should avoid reading these but since the audience will not see you, it is permissible to look through the content of the cards as you proceed through the presentation

- Speak *slowly*! Even more slowly than you would normally for a presentation

- Introduce pronounced pauses between slides so that the listeners know you have finished with that slide and are about to move onto the next

Questions and Answers session

- In a recorded webcast there will be no questions. In a live webcast there may be time at the end for the audience to pose questions

- These are usually audio questions (rather than typed)

- Answer these as you would answer in an in-person presentation but remember to speak slowly when you answer

- At the end of a live webcast, thank the participants for joining

- You can provide a contact point such as an email address if people have any further points they wish to discuss with you off-line

Dealing With The Media

You may be asked by your company or organization to appear on TV or radio. Whilst this is an exciting prospect, giving you your 15 minutes of fame, it can also be highly stressful. Even the best presenters fear this style of presentation. In part, it is because we fear they are "out to get us" and somehow trap us with their questions. We can all recall instances where a spokesperson is crucified by the interviewer, getting him or herself tied up in knots!

News is a product much like any other. It can be bought and sold. The news world is one of sound bites where long orations do not go down well. They will expect pithy answers to their questions.

More than ever before, you need to have very clear messages!

If you are invited to talk to the media, ask:

- Why have I been asked?

- What am I trying to achieve?

- What is their angle?

- Who is the audience?

- What do they think now?

- What would I like them to think?

- How can I make this happen?

Write down on an index card

- Key message 1

- Key message 2

- Key message 3

The key messages will be used to measure your success. Limit this to 3 key messages only. Before an interview on TV or radio the interviewer should run through the questions they are going to ask. It would not be fair to spring unexpected questions on you.

Hot tip

Ask the interviewer what questions you will be asked so that nothing surprises you.

Compose yourself

Try to relax and look comfortable. Sit up straight and keep your hands in your lap. Avoid looking at the camera – instead keep your eye on the person interviewing you.

Broad then narrow

Make sure your key messages are written down and close to hand when you begin the interview. When you are asked a question, begin with a broad answer then narrow down and give one or two specifics. You need to spell things out since you have an audience with very different backgrounds and variable understanding of the subject on which you are speaking.

"*What this means is ...*" provides the broad context and helps answer the "So what?" question. Next you can give examples:

"*To give you one example, let's take ...*"

Do the same for all your key points. Get the point across first using a broad statement then give an example so they really get the message.

If you are being interviewed live you will need to have your wits about you since there are no re-takes! If the interview is to be recorded and shown later then if you mess up your lines or say something you should not this can be edited out.

Summary

- PowerPoint and Keynote presentations can be livened up with the addition of video

- Links are made between the PowerPoint slide and the video file – the video is not embedded into the PowerPoint file itself. Ensure the video file and the PowerPoint file are in the same folder when you present or the video will not play

- Split projection techniques are useful for displaying text on one screen and photos, images or video on the other. The technique requires practice so avoid if you are a novice

- Telephone conference presenting is a form of virtual presentation. In order to be successful, these presentations need advance planning, an agenda and a group of people who understand the rules. Because there are no visual cues you need to be careful about what you say and how you say it

- Flip charts are useful for small informal meetings. Audience participation is encouraged, and this format suits brainstorming, planning or sales meetings

- White and blackboards are mainly used in education although whiteboards are useful to have in your office so you can write down your ideas and to-do list

- The overhead projector, despite its analog status, remains popular in schools and colleges. This is partly because they are inexpensive, but also because they encourage an interactive style of learning

- Video conferencing is big in business and is *big business*! This style of conferencing allows participants from around the world to "meet" and discuss issues as though they were all in the same room. Video conferencing is largely reserved for private industry because of its prohibitive cost

- Webcasts are excellent tools for sharing information and for e-learning. Audio and video streams are streamed live or pre-recorded and watched on participants' laptops

- Dealing with the media requires media training. You must know *why* you are being interviewed and have your key messages to hand

10 Any Questions?

The Question & Answer session is daunting for the inexperienced speaker. Learn how to handle questions well, including those from hostile questioners.

Questions From The Floor

This is a stressful part of the presentation for many people. You not only have to deliver a top class presentation to an audience, you also have to be questioned by them – in public – and presenters worry that they will not know the answers and will look foolish.

Question sessions are useful since they allow you to further reinforce your key messages. Sometimes you can bring in material that was not covered by your talk, for example *"That's a great point. We did look at that but I didn't include that information during the presentation because we only had 15 minutes. What we found was ..."*.

The question time also gives you another opportunity to show how brilliant you are – if you really know your material you should be able to handle the majority of the questions with ease. For the audience, it allows them to voice concerns over some of the issues raised in your presentation.

Questions during the presentation

In smaller meetings it is more appropriate to say *"Just interrupt as I go through this presentation – anything that doesn't make sense just let me know"*. This will undoubtedly slow you down and your perfectly crafted 30 minute talk may go on for an hour. But this usually does not matter too much in the informal setting. In terms of stress, this method of questioning is not very stressful and most of us can handle this quite easily.

Questions at the end of the presentation

This type of Question and Answer session is more typical of a large meeting such as a conference. You will be given around 15 minutes which is for the presentation and the questions. Once you show your last slide – pause – then say something like *"Thank you for your attention. I would be very happy to take questions."*

This can be more stressful since the questioners may put you on the spot, you may struggle to find the answer and suddenly things feel out of your control. You can control this situation, however, and it is worth learning a few tactics.

Tactics

- Try to identify likely questions well ahead of the presentation and design model answers for these (write them down in a notebook or on index cards if necessary)

- Remain calm – you are nearly there, you have done the hard work giving the presentation so try to enjoy the last few minutes

- Listen to the question carefully

- Thank the questioner for the question, and use his or her name if you know the person

- It is a good idea to repeat the question so that people who did not hear it will know what was being asked

- If you don't understand the question – ask for it to be repeated

- Try "*I'm not sure I caught that – are you asking ...?*"

- Pause long enough to compose the answer in your head – do not just start talking – you will look more measured if you pause briefly

- Give a short straightforward answer

- Make your answer relevant to the presentation

- It may help if you refer back to your talk or slides

- You can relate experiences "*Yes, we tried that experiment and like you, found it didn't work.*"

- Address your answer to the person asking the question but try to scan the whole room to make them feel involved

- If you don't know the answer do not feel ashamed – we cannot be expected to know everything

- Never lie

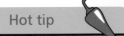

Hot tip

Listen carefully to the question and ask for it to be repeated if necessary.

You can, and should, learn how to predict questions so you are even more prepared.

Learn to Predict Questions

You can probably predict most of the questions you are likely to be asked after a presentation. Much like an exam, there are questions you just know will come up. You may have given this presentation before and will have been asked questions. Did you write these down? Have you polished the rough edges so you can answer those questions better next time?

Go through your entire presentation and try to work out what the audience might ask.

If you are selling a product they will want to know about the unmet need, patents, and longevity of the product.

If you are giving a talk on a new drug in development, the audience will want to know about the study subjects, physical properties of the molecule, interactions, side effects, and efficacy rates.

If you are giving a scientific presentation the audience may want to hear more about the methods used, whether you tried the same experiment using different methods or cell lines.

Get yourself a notebook

- Allocate one page per question

- Write down key points relating to the answer

- Then try writing a couple of short sentences bringing all this together

- Try to recall questions that have come up before – did you answer the question well? Could it have been better? Improve on the answer now, before the question is asked again

- You can re-read these notes on the way to the presentation – this will keep the answers fresh in your mind and make you look more polished

Hostile Questioners

Thankfully this does not happen too often but it is an unpleasant experience when it does. There are people who are very opinionated and who will stand up at the end of a presentation and attack the presenter verbally. It is usually just one person rather than the entire audience that acts this way, thankfully!

Some people like showing off and they may be trying to score points off you to impress their colleagues. Or they may have another agenda – maybe they do not like your company or your boss and this provides a way of getting back at them.

Can you predict hostile questions?

Sometimes you can. For example if you are planning to build a new factory right next to a residential area and you are presenting the plans to people who might be affected then they will have hostile questions for you! If you are presenting data on a new drug that is going to be very expensive you might be asked why doctors should not just use the existing cheaper treatments.

Tactics

- Do not take it personally – it is likely to be what you present, rather than you as a person, that they are attacking

- Remain calm and avoid adopting a hostile manner – this only fans the flames and makes things worse

- Ask all questioners up-front to state who they are and who they represent. This will reduce much of the inflammatory questions since they will probably not want to be identified

- Try to find areas where you agree – some common ground helps defuse things. For example, you might try *"I agree with you. This is a tricky area and I think you are right about X, but I am not sure I can agree with you about Y. But thanks for raising this. Next question."* – point to another person to take the attention off the hostile questioner

- If the questioner is dominating the floor you could say *"Thank you for your input. Could we hear from some of the other audience members who may have views on what I just presented?"*

- If it looks as though you cannot resolve it, try *"So we can hear from some other people could you and I perhaps chat after the meeting? Thanks. Next question?"*

Off-Topic Questions

Some questions come from the left-field and are clearly off-topic. It may be that the person simply has not understood what you have said and is going off at a tangent.

Alternatively, they may not have been paying attention!

Don't forget, some people like to ask questions for the sake of it, and they may be wanting to draw attention to themselves, or trying to prove a point, or maybe even want to score points off you or the organization you represent. But it is best to take all questions at face value, appear civil, and answer carefully. Appearing polite and respectful despite the nature of the questions posed will enhance your standing with the audience.

Tactics

- Try not to appear impatient even if the question is naive or way off-topic. Answer as best you can and diplomatically steer the discussion back to the main presentation

- Try to summarize the participant's viewpoint and see if you can relate this to what you were talking about – "*I am not sure that's exactly what I meant earlier but if you recall what I said about X, you might find...*"

- The issue might be an interesting one even if not directly relevant to the current discussion. Suggest that the person who asked the question wait behind till after the meeting has ended you could discuss things further then. At this point you can steer the person in the right direction and sort out any confusion without embarrassing them in public

- Alternatively you could try "*I'm not sure now is the right time to discuss this although it is something we have an interest in*"

- You can be honest and tell the audience that this is a different topic but one that is very interesting nonetheless. If it links in with what you have been talking about you can try to bridge between the off-topic question and your main topic. This does take some skill, however and you might want to avoid doing this if you are not quite sure how to get there!

- Resist the temptation to sound scornful. Instead, you can try thanking the questioner and say "*That's an interesting point. Thanks*"

Difficult Questions

What happens if someone asks us a question to which we do not know the answer? This happens to us all from time to time. We are only human and we do not know everything! In most Q & A sessions there is usually one question that we struggle to answer, and providing you are honest it really doesn't matter all that much.

Inexperienced presenters are more fazed by this than the old hands who shrug it off. Panic can set in – you have been asked something in a public forum on a topic which you should know about and yet you cannot answer this question!

Our first instinct is to fill the void by saying *something*. You do not want the audience to know you have any failings so you flail around looking for something to say.

Don't forget

Some questions are difficult to answer. You cannot know everything.

Make it up?
Absolutely not! This is sometimes a tempting option since you think you will save face simply by giving some form of answer. Unfortunately, you will probably be found out and your credibility will drop.

Tactics
"That's a really interesting point but I can't give you an answer right now. If you want, I can find out for you and get back to you?"

"You may well be right – I'm not sure I know the exact answer to that one".

Deflection techniques
Try to deflect the question on to someone else, even the questioner:

"I'm not sure – what's your opinion?"

"I'm not sure – but John Smith is in the audience and he may be able to answer this – John?"

What Was The Question?

There are some questions that you will not understand. This happens not infrequently and can be unnerving. Someone in the audience will approach the microphone, start talking and as you nod your head as he speaks you realize you haven't got a clue what he is asking! Maybe his accent is strong or the acoustics are bad, but whatever the reason, you have been thrown a question and you don't know how to start answering.

Tactics

- Take a deep breath

- Ask the questioner to use the mike if they had not used it previously

- Ask for the question to be rephrased *"Sorry, I didn't quite catch that – could you just clarify what it is you're asking? Thanks."*

- If you are still not sure, look to the chairman and see if he can help – maybe he understood the question or can say to the questioner *"We cannot understand what you are asking. Can you rephrase it for us, thank you."*

Questions within questions!

Sometimes people ask complicated questions which contain 2, 3 or more subquestions. Answering these can be tricky because often, after answering most of the subquestions, we forget the final part and have to ask the questioner to repeat.

Tactics

- Repeat the question with its subquestions for the benefit of the audience The added bonus for you is that it reinforces the question and helps you remember its various parts

- If you have a piece of paper to hand you can jot down words that will remind you of the questions being asked. Later, you can refer to this to ensure you have answered all parts of the question

- Start by saying something like *"You are asking 3 things, X, Y and Z. Let me start with X..."*.

- If you are short of time you can elect only to answer part of the question

Hot tip

Repeat back complex questions and jot down some notes as the questioner speaks.

Baptism of Fire

You will have notched up anther successful presentation and this will help boost your confidence. Hopefully you will have worked hard on your presentation before you got to this stage and, perhaps if this is a talk you have given before, you will have ironed out the rough parts, improved your slides to make them clearer, got rid of bad graphics and replaced them with good ones.

The Question and Answer session is useful since it puts you in the hot seat and people can see you perform under pressure. There may be colleagues in the audience who feel you would fit well within their organization and you might be offered a job! This does happen at meetings, often after a great presentation has been delivered.

You may be bruised after the Q & A session but you will have become more adept at handling questions, easy and difficult. This will be very useful experience for next time when hopefully you will not fear the questions or the questioners so much.

Learning points

- Annotate your speakers notes with all the questions that came up after your presentation

- Mark those that were particularly difficult

- If you did not answer these as well as you would have liked, obtain the information you need and modify your answers

- Ask your boss or colleagues who were in the audience how they might have handled the questions – is there anything they might have said differently?

- Update all the questions and answers in the notebook you have been keeping for questions and model answers

- If possible, keep a copy of the handout used for the presentation and annotate heavily. Mark those slides that were good, those that were confusing to the audience or to you, highlight areas which generate interest from the audience and expand on these sections next time you give this talk

- Remember that although you may not feel the immediate benefit, you will, over time, be better at handling the unexpected during a presentation

Summary

- Taking questions after a presentation can be stressful if you are an inexperienced speaker

- If the audience is small you can invite them to ask questions as you go through your presentation. This is useful if you are presenting complex material since people can clarify points as your proceed rather than store questions up till the end

- For large meetings such as conferences, questions are generally reserved until the end of the talk

- When asked a question, remain calm, think hard about what is being asked, repeat the question to make sure you have understood. Also, any audience members who did not hear the question will understand the answer

- If you did not hear the question, ask for it to be repeated and, if necessary, put another way so you fully understand what the questioner wants to know

- With practice you can predict most of the questions that will come up

- Write model answers for all the predictable questions so you know these by heart. Go through your presentation and imagine what *you* might ask if you were one of the audience members

- Sometimes questions and questioners can be hostile. The hostility is usually against the material or topic of the presentation – and not directed against *you* as such

- Try to remain calm in these settings and defuse the situation by finding common ground or suggesting you chat after the meeting

- Some questions are difficult and you cannot be expected to have answers for every question. If you do not know the answer – simply say so

- Sometimes you cannot understand a questioner because the acoustics are bad or because of language differences. Ask for the question to be repeated and if necessary ask the chair to help out

11 Resources

There are many resources available to help you write that great speech. The best resource is inside your head but browsing through these may help inspire you!

General Presentation Books

With the huge growth in e-learning and the Internet there are many online resources devoted to helping people present better, and improve their PowerPoint skills. It would be very difficult to list every presentation book available on the market. However, some of the better ones are listed here.

The ultimate presentation "bible" has to be *Presentation Zen: Simple Ideas on Presentation Design and Delivery* by Garr Reynolds (New Riders). The basic premise of this book is that simplicity is the key. If you keep your slides and messages simple, they will have a much greater impact than if you cram your slides full of detail. If you only buy *one* book (apart from the one you are holding, of course!) on presentation skills I would urge you to buy this. The graphics and layout are stunning. Garr Reynolds also has a great website with lots of links. If you are ever stuck for ideas for your presentation, wander over to the site *http://www.presentationzen. com/* and see how the best presenters do it.

Another inspirational book is *That Presentation Sensation* by Martin Conradi & Richard Hall (Financial Times/Prentice Hall). Rather than provide step-by-step instructions, the authors have collected stories and interviews from great presenters. You can see how they think, what they like and dislike in a presentation, what works and what does not, and you get a real feel for what makes a presentation great.

In the Spotlight: Overcome Your Fear of Public Speaking and Performing by Janet Esposito (Capstone) explores the nature of fear and anxiety and helps you find methods of reducing this.

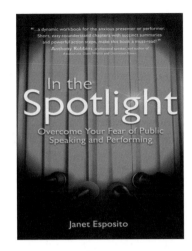

In a similar vein *Never Be Nervous Again* by Dorothy Sarnoff (Ivy Books, NY) – was written in 1987 and is now out of print. You can still obtain second-hand copies through Amazon. In this small volume, Dorothy Sarnoff helps you cope with anxiety, prepare engaging speeches, and learn how to grab and hold the audience's attention.

How to Speak Like a Pro by Leon Fletcher (Ballantine Books) provides tips for dealing with stage fright and helps you develop practicing techniques. He also includes useful tips on preparing and presenting different types of speeches.

Public Speaking in easy steps, which I have also written (In Easy Steps), provides the critical

information needed to write a compelling speech. The book is compact and written in short, easy to read sections. It will help you put together a great speech whatever the occasion. The book covers planning and organizing, using humor and other aids to ensure maximum impact, how to hone your delivery, and answer questions with confidence.

PowerPoint Resources

Start by visiting the Microsoft website where you will find tips, templates and other useful information relating to the Office suite and PowerPoint *http://office.microsoft.com/en-us/powerpoint/default.aspx*.

PowerPoint 2007 in easy steps by Andrew Edney (In Easy Steps) is a great place to start. The author is a seasoned IT guru with many years of presentation experience under his belt. Using clear and concise text alongside superb graphics he will help you put together a great set of slides that will ensure your presentation impresses!

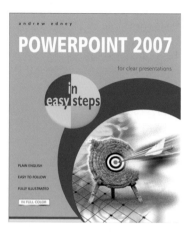

Similarly, *Solving the Powerpoint Predicament: Using Digital Media for Effective Communication* by Tom Bunzel (QUE) is a useful resource for presenters who want to explore the full multimedia capabilities of PowerPoint. This book comes with a CD containing practice presentations which you can play with and modify for your own use.

PowerPoint templates

Templates can be useful but try to avoid those with too much fussy detail. Some sites offer free templates as a means of getting you to browse through their other templates, which you can purchase. Check out *http://www.presentationpro.com*, and also PowerPoint Heaven *http://pptheaven.mvps.org*, an entertainment portal for PowerPoint animations, games, artworks, showcases, animation templates and tutorials. These sites offer downloads, tutorials, and links to other useful sites. A useful site for maximizing your PowerPoint is *http://www.presentationload.com/ index.php*.

PowerPoint Heaven

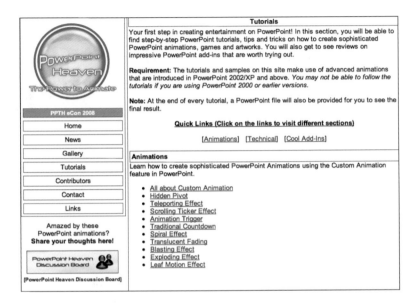

Graphicsland

This is another of the many PowerPoint template sites.

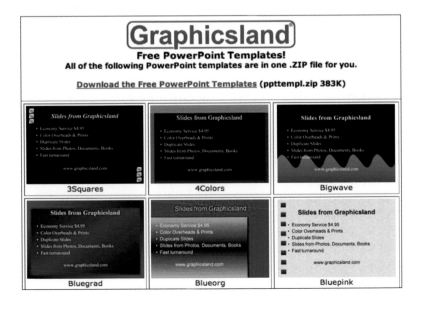

Apple Keynote Resources

Start with Apple's own site *http://www.apple.com/iwork/keynote/* which contains useful information and links.

There are one or two great books out there to help you get more from Apple's presentation software. Tom Negrino's *Keynote for MAC OS X* in the Visual QuickStart Guides range is excellent and worth reading if you plan to use Keynote for your presentation slides. Also by the same author is *Creating Keynote Presentations with iWork: Visual QuickProject Guide* (VisualQuickProject).

Online resources

Keynote Pro (*http://www.keynotepro.com/index.html*) contains tutorials and tips on using Keynote. The site offers a number of high quality themes for purchase. As with PowerPoint templates, some themes are over-fussy but there are others which are excellent and worth buying. The *Tips & Tricks* section explains how the themes are constructed, and how the masters may be modified. The company offers an RSS feed which will allow you to receive *Keynote Pro* news.

Keynote User

This site offers similar features to *Keynote Pro* and others. There is some free stuff, in addition to themes for purchase.

Alternative Free Programs

OpenOffice, NeoOffice & ThinkFree Office

Hot tip

If you cannot afford PowerPoint there are plenty of free alternatives.

These are integrated packages much like the Microsoft Office suite. However, because these are open source projects they are free of charge. Both OpenOffice and NeoOffice are available for a variety of platforms (Windows, Mac, Linux and Sun Solaris). They contain word processing software, along with a presentation package, spreadsheet, and other functions.

The programs can open and save in common formats including .doc and .ppt so you can present your slides at a meeting even if PowerPoint is used at the venue.

You can download OpenOffice at *http://why.openoffice.org/index. html*, NeoOffice at *http://www.neooffice.org/neojava/en/index.php*, and ThinkFree Office at *http://www.thinkfree.com*.

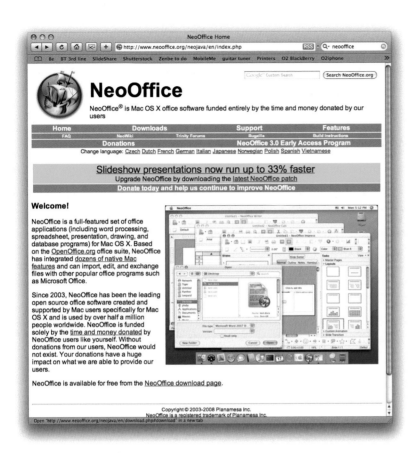

PowerPoint Viewer

If you wish to view a PowerPoint presentation but you do not have the PowerPoint program, download the free viewer from *www.microsoft.com*.

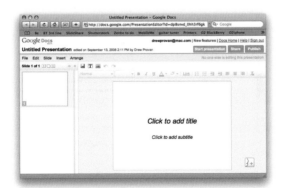

Google Docs

Google Docs is free and includes word processing, spreadsheet and presentation software. The files are online and can be accessed anywhere using any platform.

Public Speaking Websites

There are many sites offering tips for public speaking. Some are there mainly to advertise courses but there are others which do offer advice free of charge. Many of these have good content which you can read on-line or print off to read later.

TED (http://www.ted.com)

TED stands for *Technology, Entertainment, Design*. There is an annual conference attended by around one thousand participants. The material covered includes science, the arts and design, so there will be something for everyone.

The conference features speeches and presentations by inspiring presenters such as Seth Godin, Tony Robbins and Ken Robinson. The conference is sold out well in advance and is prohibitively expensive. However, free of charge, they make the best talks available to watch online. If you are looking for ways to pep up your own presentation style you would learn much from watching these pros in action! Check out the website and watch the movies or download the audio or video podcasts from the iTunes store.

Toastmasters (http://www.toastmasters.org/)

This international non-profit organization hosts meetings in 92 countries worldwide. There are no instructors, and the meetings are run by the members. The aim is to improve presentation skills and communication techniques.

Meetings are held on a weekly basis and often use informal venues such as bars or public houses.

Other sites

- *http://connect.educause.edu/Library/Abstract/ EffectiveTeachingwithPowe/43763*

- *http://www.presentersuniversity.com/*

- *http://www.impactfactory.com/gate/public_speaking_training_ course/freegate_1552-1104-88327.html#fear*

- *http://www.sethgodin.com/sg/speaking.asp*

- *http://www.slideshare.net/Toastmasters*

- *http://www.premier-presentation.co.uk/TIPS.htm*

Fonts and Type Design

You do not need to be a typography expert to create a few slides, but knowing which fonts work together will make your documents and your slides look more impressive. There are two fun books published that bring this whole subject to life.

Robin Williams is a seasoned design writer who has written several books on Mac software. Her book entitled *The Non-designer's Design Book: Design and Typographic Principles for the Visual Novice* (Peachpit Press) is a great read. She explains why some fonts look great together and others do not. She also shows you ways to improve the look of text on the page (or screen). In effect, she provides a beginner's guide to good document design.

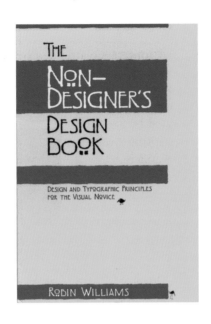

The bizarrely titled *Stop Stealing Sheep and Find Out How Type Works* by Erik Spiekermann (Adobe Press) is a superb book describing the history of type and typefaces. (The title of the book is based on a quotation by Frederic Goudy who said "*A man who would letterspace lower case would steal sheep*". This is a typographic no-no!) The book explains how fonts work, where they should be used and which work well together. There is a science behind typography as well as art!

Obtaining Great Images

Stock images

A cheap CD collection called *Nova Art Explosion Photo Objects 150,000 (Mac)* published by Avanquest Software contains a mixture of useful images with some that are not particularly great. However the CD is cheap so one cannot quibble when you get 150,000 images in one package!

Online images are more expensive and can be obtained by subscription or per image. Often the total price paid for each image depends on where the image will be used. Prices are higher for commercial books than for not-for-profit.

Shutterstock and iStockphoto

Check out Shutterstock (*www.shutterstock.com*) and iStockphoto (*www.istockphoto.com*).

Clip art

This can be obtained from many vendors, and many of these offer the clip art for free. Others charge a fee.

- *http://www.bestclipart.com/*

- *http://www.best-of-clipart.com/*

- *http://www.pointclips.com/*

- *http://www.clipart.com/en/powerpoint*

- *http://www.animationfactory.com/en/*

Index